Scribe Publications
THE FAILURE OF FREE-MARKET ECONOMICS

MARTIN FEIL was born in 1947 in Sydney. After attending university for 13 years (ten years part-time) as a scholarship boy, he got his first job in the Customs department, and then became the Industries Commission's youngest project director at the age of twenty-six.

He was eventually responsible for 11 major industry inquiries, before striking out on his own and working as an industry-policy consultant for the next 30 years. During that time he also owned trucks, warehouses, Customs bonds-stores, and container yards, and worked for the Australian Taxation Office as its only Australian independent expert on transfer pricing and profit repatriation by multinationals. He has been chairman of the Institute of Chartered Accountants' Customs committee, and the institute's representative on the tax office's transfer-pricing subcommittee.

Feil has been writing op-ed pieces for *The Age* for many years, accompanied by illustrations by John Spooner, warning of the dangers of free-market economics. This is his first book.

JOHN SPOONER is an Australian illustrator and political cartoonist who has regularly contributed to *The Age* newspaper and has also worked as a lawyer. Spooner's credits include six Stanley awards, four Walkley awards, the 1986 Fremantle Print Prize, and the 2002 Graham Perkin Award for the Australian Journalist of the Year.

To Ernie Sharkey, a first-rate economist, a legendary Customs officer, and an assistant commissioner who has helped me through my working life.

THE FAILURE OF FREE-MARKET ECONOMICS

MARTIN FEIL

with illustrations by John Spooner

SCRIBE
Melbourne

Scribe Publications Pty Ltd
PO Box 523
Carlton North, Victoria, Australia 3054
Email: info@scribepub.com.au

First published by Scribe in 2010

The publishers gratefully acknowledge the assistance of *The Age* in
supplying digital images of John Spooner's illustrations.

Typeset in 13/17 pt Garamond 3 by the publishers
Printed and bound in Australia by Griffin Press. Only wood grown
from sustainable regrowth forests is used in the manufacture of paper
found in this book.

National Library of Australia
Cataloguing-in-Publication data

Feil, Martin

The Failure of Free-Market Economics

9781921215544 (pbk.)

1. Free enterprise. 2. Australia–Economic conditions.

Other authors/contributors: Spooner, John, 1946-

330.122

www.scribepublications.com.au

Contents

Introduction

Most politicians and commentators call the financial-sector implosion of 2007–09 the global financial crisis, but it is now well beyond the crisis point. Crises occur and are overcome; this crisis is an unmitigated, unresolved, and still not fully revealed disaster, despite deceptive comments to the contrary.

This global financial disaster has been in progress since 2005, and some of its worst effects are yet to come. American commentators expect that the number of US housing foreclosures will increase from 2.4 million in 2009 to as many as eight million between 2009 and 2013. Over seven million Americans lost their jobs in the two years to December 2009.

General Motors ('What's good for General Motors is good for America') has emerged, for the time being, from a humiliating bankruptcy, and even then only after having been rescued by the US taxpayer.

Alan Greenspan, the great global champion of (and now penitent for) free-market economics, said recently that the continued slump in US home prices was putting millions of borrowers at risk. He thinks that the banks have to raise more money.

The global financial disaster will ultimately impact directly on 20 million Americans. It will damage the lives of more than a billion people in industrialised nations — they will lose substantial parts of their savings, their share values, their superannuation, their house values and, in many cases, their jobs.

In the poorer countries of the world, aid and charity work will be reduced. It is likely that the dishonest financial play by the American financial sector will result in the deaths of a large number of people.

This sounds shocking because it is. No amount of political, media, or finance-sector spin will eradicate the reality of the consequences of the global financial disaster.

Governments all over the world have been dealing with its catastrophic consequences since September 2008. Banks and many other managers of our money in deposits, superannuation, and shares are still only drip-feeding the extent of the disaster to the people who have lost the money. The big four Australian banks raised $90 billion in additional capital from the market during 2008–09, and went on to raise $10 billion more. This, of course, diluted the value of their existing shares.

Other major companies have also raised tens of billions of dollars to 'repair their balance sheets'. Macquarie Bank raised $16 billion in 2008–09.

The financial disaster began with a massive financial scam involving low-documentation housing mortgages (that is, loans with no bank account, salary, or credit-card debt information provided by the borrowers), created initially by the US mortgage marketers and then sliced, diced, expanded, and sold by the great Wall Street houses of Lehman Brothers, Goldman Sachs, and Merrill Lynch, and by financial institutions such as UBS, Credit Suisse, and Citigroup to banks, pension funds, investment funds, superannuation funds, councils, state and federal governments, and infrastructure instrumentalities and all the other keepers of the world's money.

For most of us, the unanswered questions are how and why the global financial disaster happened, how it came to Australia, and what needs to be done to repair Australia's economy. The rest of the world needs to be repaired, too, but our first priority has to be fixing up the damage done to our economy and our society.

So far, Australia has apparently fared the best of virtually all developed countries in the global financial disaster. This may be partly a reflection of the government's failure to investigate the extent of the losses. In Australia, there are no televised parliamentary inquisitions asking the Reserve Bank of Australia, the Australian Prudential Regulation Authority, the Future Fund, and the banks how much we have borrowed and how much they have written off.

The Rudd government has been scathing about the opposition's attempts to 'talk down the economy'. Negativity during a war is never well received by a government—and for good reason. Negative consumer perceptions reduce consumption, and increase savings. This is precisely what governments don't want to happen in a recession.

Our superannuation funds are urging members to deposit more, and there is a general strategy on the part of government and the big companies to argue that we may not have missed a bullet, but that we have emerged better than any other country.

This story ignores the present and future costs of the disaster to the Australian people. It is the ultimate in media spin, designed to get people to take money from under their mattresses.

People have the right to know what happened during the economic events that have had and will have direct and severe financial consequences for them and their families. In some cases, the effects will be life changing.

The Australian government's response to the global financial disaster so far has been excellent, but there is a long way to go. We have escaped the full force of the disaster by a combination of good luck and good government management and intervention.

It is not over. This financial tsunami is an economic version of the 2004 Boxing Day tsunami. Its full force will be felt when institutions, companies, people, and governments have exhausted their resources — and we should not simply sit and watch the next massive wave of losses and unemployment roll in. The epicentre of that wave is the United States, with its increasing unemployment levels and declining consumption. America is no longer the world's consumer.

Foreclosures in the period from 2010 to 2014 will damage the American economy even more than the first wave from 2006 to 2009 has done. They will cut deeper into the fabric of American society where people do have jobs and assets. These people have some savings and credit facilities, but not enough to survive job losses and the knock-on effects across the country as the economy shrinks as a consequence of defaults, mistrust, bankruptcies, and the limited availability of credit.

EASY STREET

THE FUTURE

SPOONER

THE LIFE AND DEATH STRUGGLE BETWEEN A RICH MAN AND HIS BANKER

The worst recession since the Depression of 1930 is shrinking some long-established and major employer towns and cities in the United States. The suppliers of lunches, taxis, buses, restaurants, electricity, water, entertainment, public transport, education, hospitals, financial services, and all the other service industries will be struck as their livelihoods disappear along with the factory workers, the distributors, and the other service-providers in their towns or suburbs.

World indifference to the obvious signs of an out-of-control free-market economy created the environment for the global financial disaster. In our own country, John Spooner and I have drawn and written for *The Age* newspaper for almost 20 years on issues directly relevant to what was to become the disaster that engulfed the world in 2008. There were only a few others who publicly questioned free-market theory. We have been constant opponents of free-market economics and so-called free trade. We have watched Australian manufacturing disappear, and seen Australians get further and further into debt.

Our foreign debt has been financed from overseas, even though our banks have been the front offices for the overseas lenders and credit-card providers. Until recently, our banks have almost ignored the possibility of attracting local savings. A substantial part of their liquid assets comes either from the balances of active accounts or from the unused funds of people living in retirement homes or aged-care facilities. In both cases, the banks pay very low or no interest on these deposits.

The Australian banks' ratio of loans to deposits is 153:100. This is the worst ratio in the developed world.

In 2008, at the height of the global financial crisis, the federal government felt compelled to guarantee all deposits held by Australian-owned banks. This commitment meant that, if a bank defaulted, the government would pay back the amount of deposits held by its customers. There was no ceiling on the guarantee, although there was a charge imposed on individual deposit amounts of more than a million dollars.

The banks were also given a helping hand by the Future Fund, which is owned and funded by the Australian government. It was originally funded with a cash pile of $60 billion and a major tranche of Telstra shares owned by the government, and the Howard government had committed to handing over most of any budget surplus to the fund. The purpose of the fund was to earn a sufficient income by 2020 to allow the government to pay federal public-sector superannuation commitments that would otherwise have had to be funded directly from public resources.

This means that, in the present crisis, the banks have been greatly assisted by the government: directly, by the guarantee; and indirectly, by loans from the Future Fund. At the time of writing, the banks held $34 billion in cash that the fund had not invested.

The general attention-deficit syndrome experienced by most of us when economic debates arise is the fault of economist authors rather than their readers. Most economics texts are so dense, technical, and boring that only those who are required to read them bother to do so.

We have been lulled into a false sense of security by the federal and state governments' claims that Australia has no debt because governments of the past 20 years erased their debt by selling major public assets. This piece of ideological spin has ignored the monstrous size of Australia's private foreign debt on the grounds that it has been incurred by individuals acting rationally in their own interest, and therefore isn't a problem.

The standard political propaganda during this time has been that we are a rich, debt-free country. The illusion of a glut of wealth created by constant budget surpluses dulled our senses.

This book is meant to be a wake-up call. It distils 40 years of a working life spent arguing about trade and industry-policy issues that determine how we live and what we will leave to our children.

A great number of people have already been damaged by the 'worst recession in 75 years'. But, in my view, this is only the beginning: the recession and its aftermath will change our lives and the lives of those we love. We have yet to face the spectre of part of our population being permanently impoverished and jobless without any prospect of recovery, even after the global crisis has passed.

Ultimately, this disaster is the product of an economic theory that grew in strength from the 1970s until it became the conventional economic wisdom for universities, the media, politicians, governments, and the financial press. That theory began as economic rationalism and then became free-market economics.

Free-market economics, at its most extreme, allows government virtually no role in a mature market economy. Education, the police, defence, water, and roads are all functions that might be initiated by individuals or alliances of individuals. According to this approach, the only possible function of government is to intervene in the event of market failure.

The concept, initially known as Reaganomics, was a creation of the American right, but was made more palatable by the British Labour prime minister Tony Blair and the United States's Democrat president Bill Clinton's commitment to a third way between free-market economics and government intervention. Similarly, Labor prime ministers Hawke and Keating blunted Labor opposition in Australia to the notion of a rampant services-led economy.

The grave danger we now face is a consequence of us having allowed the economist tribe to use simple all-or-nothing assumptions, and a special language and mathematical modelling that only they understand, to enrich and empower themselves and those who used them. As is now becoming evident, they did not empirically test their assertions and models; at the same time, they rejected any criticism of their ideas based on real events in the market.

From around 1990 onwards, Australians and Australian governments stopped watching and thinking for themselves, and started uncritically accepting the hidebound economic pronouncements of 'experts' that were disseminated by a compliant media.

As a result, in the past two years, the slavish application of one strand of economic theory — free-market economics — has cut our superannuation savings by 20 per cent, destroyed 40 per cent of our share values, reduced our dividends and, in the extreme, has made some of us unemployed or forced us to work longer than we wish.

After the 2009–10 budget was handed down, Ken Henry, the secretary of the Australian Treasury, said in a speech at the National Press Club that the modelling of projections by Treasury had probably 'exceeded the reading age' of many who disagreed with its conclusions. This expressed the Brahmin-type attitude of Canberra economists that I detest. We should never accept being told to shut up while our betters do what they think is good for us.

Simplicity and clarity in explaining complex concepts are defining characteristics of intellectual quality. Obscurity and prolixity are usually signs of intellectual mediocrity or weakness.

I've seen this at work in the real world. I've been a senior partner in two first-tier accounting firms, and was responsible for a national business unit in each of them; I was the youngest project director (in 1975) in the forerunner to what is now the Productivity Commission; and I've been an adviser to any number of multinational firms and industry associations, and an independent expert to the Australian Taxation Office on the vexed question of international profit-shifting by multinationals. I have owned a number of cross-border logistics companies, including consultancies, container transport, Customs bonds, container storage yards, and a large Customs brokerage.

My company also owned a share in the Titleist golf franchise for Australia and New Zealand.

My earliest work experience was with my father and his men in his steel-fabrication business from the age of nine. It's probably because of this background that I have always wanted to understand how industries and businesses work.

This book seeks to demystify an exotic and unnecessarily complicated area of business and market knowledge. In the process, it explains why the global financial disaster was not simply bad luck or bad timing. In my view, it was the inevitable, corrupt product of hubris and selfishness in the economic policy-making and financial sector of our society.

Many of the senior people in the sector regarded the rest of society with contempt, and arbitrarily dismissed our views and marginalised our input into the conduct of our own economy.

This bullying culture impacted heavily on the rest of the world. Its practitioners believed in thought leadership: academic economists were dismissive of factual problems, while free-market economists captured the politicians in the major political parties in Britain, America, and Australia.

The economists were also manipulated by special interests such as the mining industry and right-wing ideologues, which considered that government intervention would cost them money.

After the global financial disaster, it should be obvious that we can't afford any longer to take economic theories, models, and projections on trust. They must be tested in the same way that medical researchers, engineers, and scientists test their hypotheses—against reality.

The proof of hypotheses is an essential task in every field of knowledge. In economics, there has been no attempt at proof;

instead, there has been a very casual approach to the inclusion of dynamic as well as static assumptions in economists' models. The profession has not grown and developed in the last hundred years: it still genuflects at the theoretical altars of Adam Smith, Joseph Schumpeter, and Milton Friedman.

And we are all paying the price.

Chapter One
The Making of a Maverick

We used to be able to make anything in Australia. In the post-war period from the 1950s until the early 1980s, Australia was a country that prided itself on its self-sufficiency in manufacturing. We had an electronics industry, an electrical-products industry, a capital-equipment and machinery industry, a white-goods industry, a paper and paper-board industry, 2000 timber mills, an electrical consumer-goods industry, food processing and beverage manufacture, and textiles, clothing and footwear industries. We manufactured chemicals and plastics, sporting goods, iron- and steel-based heavy engineering, non-ferrous primary shapes, and motor vehicles.

We even added value to our minerals and agricultural products, and met most of domestic market demand. BHP was the largest company in the country, and employed over 70,000 people.

We had no current-account deficit. The banks had no international debt. People saved money in bank accounts, and were paid an interest amount that they valued. Most people didn't own shares. Superannuation wasn't even thought of: the aim was to own your own home and to retire with the pension.

In October 1964, in the middle of this idyllic era, I turned 17 and met the girl who I was to marry four years later. I was living with my father and his girlfriend, but it was a silent and uncomfortable time. Dad was never home, and his girlfriend was only seven years older than me. So I spent most of my university years in the conversational heaven of my girlfriend's extended family at Concord in New South Wales. They fed me and listened to me.

In those days, working-family homes were a wonderful amalgam of mothers, fathers, uncles, aunties, grandmothers, and grandfathers all living together. The most common entertainment was to be found around the kitchen table.

In 1965, I had promised my girlfriend's uncle Kelvin a boat trailer for Christmas. There was one small problem: I didn't know how I was going to keep my promise. I confessed this to my father on Christmas Day itself, after one of Dad's legendary Christmas Eve work parties, when he had a major hangover.

He owned a steel fabrication and construction company that employed 200 boilermakers, ironworkers, and riggers. Dad certainly believed in the totalitarian maxim of Essington Lewis, BHP's famous chief executive: 'I am work.' Everything else and everyone else (except me) were incidental. Dad spent most of his time at work, and generally came home drunk.

He had started work at the age of 14, catching rivets on the Sydney Harbour Bridge construction site. The rivets were red hot, and if you dropped a catch they could do a lot of damage. The next time you cross the Harbour Bridge, have a look at the tens of thousands of rivets in the columns.

That Christmas morning, Dad didn't say anything. We just went to his works, which were closed for the holidays. There, I watched him heat, bend, cut, and weld steel to create a boat trailer of commercial quality without using a template, drawings, or anything else that a modern-day handyman would rely on. In those days, our tradesmen were that good. The trailer was finished in about three hours.

Dad and the men who worked with him (not just for him) could do anything with steel. The elite group were boilermakers who had completed five-year apprenticeships, during which time they earned very little money. They became craftsmen in steel. They were a polyglot collection of Germans, Italians, and displaced Europeans who smoked, drank beer, and worked hard — just like Dad. They were strong, harsh men with dirty nails, and with grit ingrained in their hands.

My father and mother separated in their early thirties. Mum had five children, and I was the only boy. We moved around a lot, and a new school always meant that I was involved in fights. I think that she got tired of other boys' fathers turning up to talk to my father and being told that he wasn't there.

My sisters stayed with Mum, and I lived with Dad from the time I was seven until I married at the age of twenty-one. As I've said, he worked and drank. We lived in hotels with relatives, and in houses and flats with different women. I attended 12 different schools, and read and read. There was nothing else to do in the hotel room; there was no television, and you had to put threepence in the wireless to make it work. We lived at the Olympic Hotel near Hyde Park in Sydney for a long time.

Linda, the publican's wife, was the only person I can

remember giving me a cuddle in those days. I saw Mum about every six months, and even then she would only let me into the house if I went straight into a bath.

I went to four public schools while I was still with Mum. Then I went to the Little Sisters of St Joseph at Leichhardt, where the nuns used the cane to try to make me write right-handed. They were unsuccessful. I boarded at the De La Salle Brothers' Oakhill College when I was ten, and then went to the same Brothers' establishment at Lakemba. I spent my thirteenth year in a Capuchin seminary at Plumpton, and went to the Patrician Brothers at Blacktown. I then went back to Lakemba, and finally boarded with the Christian Brothers at Waverley.

The father of my clever, lifelong friend Freddy Lahood owned the snooker room at Campsie. I used to go home with Freddy most afternoons and play snooker. We soon graduated to billiards, a more interesting game.

My major schooling was at St John's at Lakemba, a working-class suburb in the Western part of Sydney, from year five to year ten. Dad and I then settled down for a couple of years at Canterbury, an inner-west suburb, where we lived with my father's mother. Nearly every day I got off the train at the adjoining of suburb of Campsie, went to Freddy's place, and walked home to Canterbury. I organised my own dinner.

Dad didn't care where I was, and generally came home after I was in bed. I didn't wash very often in my early teenage years, which probably explains Mum's attitude. She was a cleanliness fanatic, or at least seemed like one to me.

Freddy's mother, Vickie, was one of the sharpest, smartest, kindest people I have ever met. She came from a generation of women who never had the chance to go to university, but who were a lot smarter than most of the men who did. We spent most afternoons arguing about religion, life, and everything that wasn't mundane. She certainly taught me to hunger for knowledge, and to refuse to accept illogical arguments, no matter who uttered or wrote them.

Vickie Lahood died of cancer in her late fifties. A week before she died, she asked Fred what if, when she got to heaven, I turned out to have been right, and there was a pagan, god-like Buddha waiting for her at the pearly gates instead of the Christian Trinity. Few Catholic women of her generation had the capacity to admit that possibility on the basis of a conversation with a 14-year-old, or to be amused by the idea. Her uncomplicated, pure faith was a beautiful thing to see.

For a long time, the Lahoods' place was the closest I had to a home.

I could weld and use an oxyacetylene torch by the time I was nine. I worked with the boilermakers, the riggers, and the ironworkers, and in the office where the templates were made and the bolt lists were made up. Dad did the estimating and quotations. His father was German, and Dad had some very Germanic traits. For example, his price was his price; it was not an invitation to bargain. The engineers used to enjoy ringing him up and asking him to sharpen his pencil. Dad never changed a price, but he abused a lot of pencil-sharpening engineers.

From the age of 13, I worked during every school holidays, either with Dad or with firms of draftsmen or engineers that gave him work. There were no tennis camps and cricket schools then. I only realised later that Dad was, for most of the time, a working single parent whose day lasted from six in the morning until ten at night. He had no one else to mind me.

The best men to work with were those who erected the fabricated-steel skeletons of the buildings — the riggers. Their hands and arms were so strong that they could shimmy up the columns to bolt up the rafters and purlins (horizontal, roof-long support beams). I had to be lifted up to the roof on the hook of the crane, or balance myself on the steel being lifted. No one thought about occupational health and safety in those days. Some of the riggers literally ran along the steel rafters placing the bolts for the purlins, which were erected 20 or 30 metres in the air. My job was to tighten the nuts on the bolts. The riggers would come behind me, and give each nut a few extra twists.

If we were erecting a building away from Sydney, we stayed in pubs. I went to bed while the men drank. They had a gypsy lifestyle that involved little self-examination or thought about the future.

At country building sites early in the morning, the steel was freezing — it felt as if your hands were sticking to the metal. My coldest memories are of helping to erect the first hotel at Smiggin Holes in the New South Wales snowfields and a building in Queanbeyan, near Canberra.

I had known Dad's workers for as long as I could remember. They were his friends, and we used to go to their homes for dinner. I can still see their faces, and speak their names. They taught me that English was a living language, and that not all the words had found their way into the Oxford English Dictionary. They also taught me the value of adjusting what you said and how you spoke to the vocabulary, rhythms, cadence, and tones of your audience, and to their interests.

After I sat for the Leaving Certificate in 1964, I won a Commonwealth Scholarship to Sydney University. Before me, no one in my extended family had got as far as the Intermediate Certificate (the present-day equivalent is the School Certificate).

My one strong memory from that time is going to Kings Cross to get the exam results. The newspapers used to paste the results on a board at 1.00 a.m. I was so excited that I jumped over a Volkswagen in William Street at the Cross. I loved to high jump in those days. I had steel-wire muscles, weighed 64 kg, and was 192 cm tall, with a spring in my step. The jump was easier than the exams.

I started an Arts–Law degree at Sydney University. Dad had thought I would study Engineering, and join him in his business. Of course, we hadn't talked about it at the time; I didn't even contemplate what he wanted. He had never expressed his feelings or his hopes for me. There had been no discussion about my future.

I had no personal knowledge of university, and so didn't think about or hope for any further education. I liked examinations and devoured books, but had no thought of a career. I realise now that my personality, as I grow older, seems more and more like my father's: I have a curious ability to plan for the future, and yet to live in the present.

I was the only son, and Dad had shared his life and his work with me. Some nights when he came home, he woke me up to show me the drawings for his latest job or to talk to his friends and show them how much I knew about the steel fabrication and construction business.

Dad worked until he was seventy-nine. He only stopped when the computer-using engineers stopped asking him to quote. The pencil-sharpening engineers had retired by then.

Dad's ultimate response to my destruction of his ambitions

for me was to stop feeding me and giving me work. This meant that I had to find outside work, and therefore couldn't enter the Law faculty. In those days, Law only provided daytime lectures; part-time students were unheard of. It was possible to get time off work to attend lectures for one subject, but this meant that I would have had to take ten years to complete a law degree part-time.

I switched to the Economics faculty, and then spent nine years part-time in that dismal faculty anyway. I wouldn't have started had I known the future—but then I would have missed the life and work experience that I've had.

Economics was a relatively new discipline in those days. The scientists, doctors, lawyers, and engineers certainly regarded it as no more than a jumped-up Arts degree, with little of the intellectual rigour that it now claims to possess. The economists have certainly exacted their revenge for that accurate slight.

***

I started work in the Department of Customs and Excise in January 1968, where my first job was as a clerk in the personnel section. The personnel officer was a young fellow called Francis Ivor Kelly, who was very sharp and personable. Frank was to go on to become the first comptroller-general of Customs with no university qualifications, and the first Customs officer to become the permanent head of the department.

Previous chief executives of Customs had been appointed from Trade and Industry. The prevailing view was that Customs personnel needed to have some idea of the origins of and the policy reasons for the legislation they were responsible for. Frank broke a very old mould.

Customs was the very essence of a Catholic tribe. The Post Office was the same. In those days, there was no point in working in either department unless you were a Catholic. In other departments, the reverse was true: there was no point working in them unless you were a Protestant and, preferably, a Mason. Otherwise, you simply didn't get on. In the first section of Customs I worked in, any Protestants found eating a meat pie on a Friday at lunch were castigated by the assistant personnel officer.

Girls who got married were asked to leave the Commonwealth Public Service; not surprisingly, there were no senior women employed. The women who were tolerated worked as typists, steno-secretaries, and comptometer operators. (Comptometers were very large mechanical calculators, not far removed from an abacus.)

You were expected to work for Customs until you retired, and the department was a career island — no one was appointed to Customs from other departments until the 1990s. Even an abortive attempt to recruit fresh senior blood from industry in the early 1990s resulted in the ostracism of and ultimate retreat by anyone foolish enough to think they could have a middle-level career in Customs coming from somewhere else. Those sent to private enterprise on exchange seldom came back.

Customs was also a seriously hard-drinking department. The hotels around Circular Quay were the Customs House, the First and Last, the Ship In, the Brooklyn, and the North British. A 'Customs Lunch' was six schooners. If you worked overtime, you had another six in the meal break.

After work in those days, a group of about ten officers

would stand in a circle having a 'shout', which meant that each drinker would, in turn, buy a drink for everyone else. You stayed until it was your turn to shout, shouted the entire group, and had to keep up with the hardened, older drinkers who poured the beer straight down their throats. It made me ill, so I gave up going to the pubs. I simply couldn't drink the quantity required.

I stopped drinking and didn't drink again until I was thirty. I was also promoted very quickly, and so was ostracised by the troops as a 'brown nose'.

My Customs career changed direction when I became a training officer. It was necessary for training officers to visit every branch and section of Customs to be able to gain a broad view of how the department operated. No one in Customs seemed to know anything about the policies and law underpinning the operations of the department. We talked about our first function as 'protecting and maintaining Australian industry', but I didn't know how we were expected to deliver the first function of Customs, and neither did anyone else.

The main policy-mechanism for protecting Australian industry was a tax imposed on imported goods, which was collected as they came into Australia by either land or air. This tax, which was called a tariff, was usually a percentage of the value of the imported goods. That value, in turn, was based on definitions in the Customs Act. The amount collected was called a duty.

In some cases, the tariff was a fixed amount plus a percentage of the value of the goods. For example, transistor radios were subject to a tariff of $10 plus 45 per cent. For cheap items, such as a transistor that might have cost $2.00

when shipped from Hong Kong in the late 1960s, the Customs tariff was equivalent to a percentage tax of 525 per cent ($10.90 compared with the original $2.00). As if that weren't enough, a sales tax was collected as well. Sales tax, like the GST that eventually succeeded it, was a tax on the consumer. It was rebatable at previous transaction-stages in the supply chain. It was based upon the import value, plus duty and other logistics costs, plus a mark-up of 20 per cent, to arrive at a value for sales-tax collection at rates of up to a further 30 per cent. This all meant that, even before the transistor got to the shops, and had distribution and retail profit-margins added on, the Customs duty and the sales tax payable had multiplied the original cost of the item by seven.

Believe it or not, even though Customs was responsible for collecting the duty and sales tax on imported goods, no one in the department knew how duty rates were established. We had no idea of the role of the Tariff Board.

The other major protective mechanisms were quotas, which limited the volume or value of goods of a particular class or kind that could be imported. Quotas were to become very important in the 1980s in the passenger motor-vehicle, and textiles, clothing, and footwear industries, as they delivered a predetermined share of the market to Australian manufacturers.

My last job in Customs was as 'Inspector, Organisation'. There were 5000 people working in the department, and there were departmental empires everywhere. My job was to convince the Commonwealth Public Service Board of the need for us to have more staff and higher-level positions. There were lots of competitive submissions, but I was good at them. I was also good at understanding and packaging the mysteries of Prevention and Detection, Inland Services, and Outport Functions at Newcastle, Port Kembla, Eden, and Coffs Harbour, and representing them appropriately to the Public Service Board. I could sell refrigerators to Eskimos.

By now, there were opportunities available to me to go to Canberra permanently within Customs, or to Paris, where I could work in the Organisation for Economic Co-operation and Development for two years. But I wanted to stay on the promotional fast track. I applied for and got a job as a project officer in a mysterious place called the Tariff Board.

Chapter Two
Wreaking Havoc at the Tariff Board

The Tariff Board had been established in 1921 as an outcome of World War I, when the Australian government realised just how remote the country was from the manufacturing centres of Europe and the United States. (Asia wasn't even thought of as a manufacturing location at this time.) The attitude was that, if we were isolated by a major European war, we needed to be able to produce the manufactured goods that we required. Defence was to remain a substantial component in the argument for industry assistance until the 1970s.

The board had been created to move the constant stream of requests from industry for assistance — mostly seeking protection against import competition through Customs duties, called tariffs — out of the back rooms of political patronage into the light of public inquiries that could be attended by all participants in an industry, and produce public reports that could be read by anybody. (The Productivity Commission is the latest incarnation of the board.)

I was 26 years old when I joined the board in 1974 as a

project officer. What followed at the macro level is instructive. Prime minister Gough Whitlam, having slashed tariffs by 25 per cent, changed the board's name to the Industries Assistance Commission. But this Orwellian ruse didn't work: the body was soon nicknamed the Industries Assassination Commission. So, as happens in such matters, the word 'Assistance' was dropped from the title. It subsequently became the Productivity Commission when it was decided, quite rightly, that it had little to do with helping industry. (There is now only one misleadingly descriptive word left to discard in its title: the next step, I suppose, is for it to be renamed the Commission.)

The chairman of the commission was Godfrey Alfred Rattigan. He was a very bright and charming man of Irish extraction. Of course, he duly refused a knighthood, which were freely available to the powerful heads of government departments in the 1960s.

Rattigan also had great determination and a vision of a more productive and competitive Australia. Upon becoming chairman of the Tariff Board in 1963, he was the person responsible for waking the board up from the protective torpor it had been in since its creation. He sold the government on the need to review all manufacturing-industry tariffs, beginning with those that had the highest rates and were the least efficient. In the process, he made the revitalised version of the board, the Industries Assistance Commission, the most important economic-policy adviser to government. He battled the Country Party's 'Black' Jack McEwen, who was the protectionist minister for industry and commerce in the Menzies era, and a very strong minded and clever man in his own right.

Alf Rattigan was the change agent who set Australia on an economic-policy course that really only finished in the late 1990s and still influences policy today. He had the charming ruthlessness that single-minded, clear-thinking leaders often have. He also had the leadership to inspire his staff. He was a truly charismatic man.

Businessman and manufacturer Ernest Rodeck told me this story of his first meeting with Rattigan:

> I was president of the Melbourne University Business School Association at the time and had to find a speaker for one of our meetings. Rattigan was in the news and I was lucky to get him.
>
> His talk was revolutionary for the time. 'Tariffs should not exceed 25 per cent', he pronounced. 'We must cut them back.' He went on to explain the now well-known theory of the level playing field. When question time came, there was deadly silence. I broke it by asking, 'But what would you do about the unemployment that would surely result?' His answer was immediate and sharp. 'That is not my department.'

Rattigan was a zealot, but he needs to be considered in the context of his time and the conventional wisdom that he fought against. Protection of industry was the name of the game until the 1970s. Tariff 'equilibration', as the board called it, was the stock policy approach.

This meant that the government created such substantial tariffs that the duty-paid prices of goods were, at best, no lower than local prices, and were often higher. As there was no real price competition, imports needed to be significantly better than the local product in terms of quality or performance to warrant their purchase by consumers.

This philosophy obviously led to a lot of cosy deals with the unions and a lazy approach, in some cases, to the need for process improvement and increased productivity in Australian manufacturing industries. But the practice of equilibration was abandoned once the tariff reductions began to bite. In the meantime, the old model was still very much in vogue in most developed countries. While we lived under the delusion that we and New Zealand had the only protected manufacturing industries in the world, it wasn't that different in most major countries.

After the flush of enthusiasm created by the manufacturing reviews and Whitlam's endorsement that he was 'a Rattigan man', the commission became a very strong participant in the industry-policy debate through its focus on manufacturing-industry reviews and the importance of tariffs and quotas in the 1970s and 1980s.

Manufacturing companies originally came along to the commission's reviews of their industries with an open mind. They were prepared to accept the discipline created by import competition. They weren't prepared, however, for their businesses to be annihilated and their business strategies criticised as being hopelessly inefficient by people who had absolutely no empirical experience and were in no position to make informed judgements about them.

My first project at the Tariff Board was an inquiry concerning the New Zealand–Australia Free Trade Agreement. (NAFTA was the predecessor of the 1988 Closer Economic Relations agreement between the two countries, which is our only true bilateral free-trade agreement.) The inquiry concerned steam and other vapour-generating boilers, communication transceivers, and cast-iron v-pulleys.

I had to find out who wanted to give evidence at the inquiry, visit their factories and meet them, write a pre-inquiry report, and generally inform the commissioner (George Johnson, an ex-senior public servant in the Department of Trade and Industry) about the industry in Australia and the market for its products.

I then had to organise the public inquiry, and prepare questions for the commissioner. The commissioner heard evidence under oath, and cross-examined the witnesses. He had the same powers as a judge of the High Court. It was a very legalistic process.

Finally, I wrote the report and draft recommendations for final approval by the commissioner, who either changed what I wrote or held further meetings to modify them before submitting them to the government.

At that time, most of the commission staff were flat out on the various product groups included in the electronics-industry review, which ultimately resulted in the virtual closure of manufacturing in what was until then a major Australian industry.

I was left entirely to my own devices. I think the assistant commissioner for the Sydney office, David Morton, decided I was a goer who could write. He told me that only four people in the Sydney office (with its professional staff of 60) could write. I never reported to anyone again in the commission, other than the commissioners and the assistant commissioner responsible for the Sydney office. I became a project director within nine months of joining what was then the Tariff Board.

During my time at the commission, I was the project director for 11 inquiries, including two NAFTA inquiries: inquiries into iron and steel, high-alloy steels, stress-relieved strand-wire cable; non-ferrous primary shapes; paints, varnishes, and lacquers; primary and storage batteries; and a Temporary Assistance Authority inquiry in which the manufacturers were seeking quotas to limit imports of colour televisions. It was heady stuff for a young man in his mid-twenties.

I believed completely in what we were trying to do. I was young, green, and idealistic. The idea of making industries outward looking, competitive, and export oriented seemed like a common-sensical and clear-thinking way to improve Australia's competitiveness. I had yet to understand the difference between what people said and what happened in the market place. I had no doubt that tariff reductions would be transmitted directly to the consuming Australian public.

This naivety prevailed in the commission. We didn't understand the subtleties of legislation that required sellers to pass on reductions in sales tax under the passing-on provisions of the Sales Tax Assessment Acts, but allowed them to keep all or most of the duty reductions. The much older Customs Act (1901) did not contemplate progressive duty reductions or deal with the subsequent question of who got the windfall money that was no longer paid in duty and tax.

(By the way, there are still no provisions that require importer or wholesaler beneficiaries of duty reductions to pass on the benefit to the consumer. There is no commercial reason for them to do so, either, so long as a rogue importer doesn't break from the herd and lower its prices—because then all the importers would have to pass on the benefit, or else lose sales to their competitor. The result of all this is that importers always keep the windfall if they aren't forced to give it up: they only pass on some of their financial gain from the tariff reduction when the reduction is enormous.)

Commission calculations of consumer benefits were always theoretical. They never surveyed the market to calculate the actual retail-price impact of a tariff reduction. They had no idea of the extent of the difference between the mark-up of the import price for the calculation of duty and the mark-up to determine a retail price.

The presiding commissioner on iron and steel was Dick Boyer, whose father, Sir Richard Boyer, had been the chairman of the ABC. He was joined by Keith Sinclair and Peter Robinson who had been, respectively, the managing editors of *The Age* and the *Australian Financial Review*.

I was sent to Melbourne by Dick Boyer in 1975 to tell the general managers of BHP that we were thinking of recommending that the government nationalise the steel industry. I still cringe at the thought that I was ignorant and insensitive enough to deliver such a message.

Steel-making was BHP's biggest activity. Their policy was to make steel out of iron ore and coal, rather than to export those raw materials. They regarded themselves as manufacturers integrated backwards into their own sources of supply—exports only occurred when they had overestimated demand from the local market.

At that time, neither Treasury nor commission economists were regarded as messiahs. They were seen, rather, as strange young men participating in the industry-policy debate who were expected to learn what industries and markets actually did. There was no developed econometric modelling or analysis being undertaken by business or the bureaucracy. Even econometrics was a new subject in the universities of the early 1970s. The Industries Assistance Commission was expected to find out what was happening in the industry under review. Its charter was to enquire and report its findings to government, so we had to come up with details of the state of the industry, its history, its finances, its technology, its competitors, and its market share over a given time-period.

Yet, despite its limitations, the commission brought to its inquiries an economy-wide perspective and independence that was beyond most businesses. Instead, most focused on their company interests or, occasionally, their industry's interests.

BHP men had grown up with Essington Lewis, BHP's managing director who had been Australia's director of supply during World War II. He was the man who had that sign on his desk which read: 'I am work.' I really knew nothing about such people. As young men on the rise, they had been required to wear a dinner suit when they dined with the managing director.

I met with 20-or-so of the senior executives (mostly general managers of various divisions and state manufacturing mills) in BHP's boardroom on about the 30th floor in Collins Street, Melbourne. The view was spectacular for someone who was used to the second floor of the Customs House at Circular Quay in Sydney.

The executives were grey-haired veterans who had moved through the company ranks in the 30 years since World War II had ended. They sat in beautifully carved chairs, around a long, elegant, antique table, and listened politely and quietly as I, a callow kid, delivered a message that I couldn't explain or justify.

The sad thing is that they didn't say anything to contradict the message or confront the messenger. I was a naive barbarian, eager to learn. My mind was open to any argument that the industry might make for the continuation of high levels of tariff protection. I wanted to learn as much as I could about the company that was then the largest employer in the country and the number-one company measured by its valuation in the stock market. But they understood that there was a new power in the land that could adversely impact their relationship with government. They wanted to appease the new Industries Assistance Commission.

We wanted to stop government intrusion in the market and the distortions created by the tariff system, but the government was creating a new form of industry assistance through direct financial payments. Years later, in 1983, BHP received about $700 million from the Hawke government as a trade-off for tariff reductions in the first of the Button Plans.

My project team went around Australia to all the BHP manufacturing and some of the mining sites. It was a journey into a business world that is long gone. The general managers of Newcastle and Port Kembla ruled empires of 10,000 and 20,000 workers. The young mill superintendents went to the Newcastle Club or the Cottage at Port Kembla, and kept their coats on until after the loyal toast.

During our visits, there were formal dinners with the BHP chief executive officer, Jim McNeil, and the executive general manager of the steel division, Brian Loton, that only the commissioners were invited to attend. They were told to bring a dinner suit for these occasions. Our team wore business suits, and were entertained by the mill managers and superintendents. We played a form of snooker with them that had been brought to Australia by the Lysaght family, who had started the Port Kembla steel works.

As we moved around the BHP facilities, I remember

standing 30 metres away on a raised platform near the mouth of a blast furnace. I could feel my eyebrows burning off. I asked how the men, who were straddling the molten metal to push slag into the waste pit, could stand the heat. The superintendent's response was that they were used to the heat. The labourers were five metres from the furnace mouth.

In the same vein, the steel-pipe rolling mills of Tubemakers, the BHP subsidiary at Port Kembla, worked with a production-line process whereby pipes rolled down a series of cambered lines at various stages of completion. The clanging noise was, literally, deafening. It really hurt your ears. The workers were supposed to wear earmuffs, but many didn't. It was a choice between a working world of silence or occupational deafness.

A lot of men died at the steel works in those days. They fell into blast furnaces filled with molten metal that was heated to above 450 degrees centigrade. They were hit by white-hot cobbles that spasmodically jumped from the conveyer belts in the rolling mills. A cobble was a stream of metal up to 40 metres long, which killed anyone unfortunate enough to be in its erratic path.

At the public hearings, the evidence of the Metal Workers Union included a list of 18 men who had died in the Port Kembla mills in a period of 12 months. Dick Boyer said, 'We will take that as read.' The union quietly accepted his direction without protest.

Ernie Sharkey said that he would have insisted on reading out every name. Ernie was my great friend, mentor, and colleague for more than 30 years through my various career changes. He was the assistant commissioner for New South Wales when he resigned from the commission in 1980 to join me in our consultancy business.

It was a great education, but it was privileged. Industry never confronted the commission. We lived in a cocoon of righteousness and entitlements. As a director, I flew business class (both Qantas and Ansett had a business-class service to Canberra in those days that served a hot breakfast on china plates), and was picked up and delivered from my home to the airport and back in a Commonwealth car or a hired Mercedes Benz.

The companies took the commission exercise very seriously. BHP submitted 12 volumes of evidence that cost them $750,000 to prepare. Their six witnesses included the chief executive officer, the executive general manager, and Henry Bosch, who was the general manager of Tubemakers (and, later, the commissioner for trade practices).

Dick Boyer ruled the inquiry with an iron fist: he tolerated no dissension or levity in the public hearings. I remember him asking Henry Bosch why he was smirking during one exchange.   ·

Dick used to go to the Hansard reporters at the end of the day and touch up the verbatim reports of the exchanges between the commissioners and the witnesses. Thus he never lost an argument. The commission ended up recommending tariff reductions, but they weren't implemented until the Button Plan for the steel industry was introduced some years later.

My next major foray was as director of an inquiry set up to determine whether quotas or high duty rates should be imposed on colour television sets, which were just being introduced into the Australian market.

In 1975, a colour TV set cost Australian families between

$700 and $1000 (probably about $3500 to $5000 at today's average earnings' levels). We conducted a temporary assistance inquiry that lasted for 45 days, and we heard from 80 witnesses, including some overseas manufacturers.

I went to Canberra and stayed at Brassey House, working 16 hours a day, seven days a week, for the entire period. Peter Robinson was the commissioner acting as the Temporary Assistance Authority. I was told that if we didn't impose quotas, the unions would keep the imported TVs on the wharves. We didn't, and they didn't.

There were about 13 manufacturers of colour TVs when they were introduced into Australia. After a few years there were only three; then there were none. It was really an assembly industry that imported over 90 per cent of the factory cost of a TV set in components. It was a perfect case to demonstrate the power of effective-rates analysis and the fact that many duties protected very little value-adding activity within Australia.

The manufacturers/assemblers asked for quotas to be imposed on imported TV sets, as well as a duty rate of 45 per cent on them. But we found that this meant the local industry was seeking a massive level of effective assistance on the small value-added Australian component involved in assembling the sets. For example, if it cost $600 to make a colour TV set locally, more than $500 of that cost was absorbed in payments for imported components such as the chassis, the picture tube, the printed circuit board, and all the capacitors and resistors soldered to the board. If we had accepted the manufacturers'/ assemblers' submission, an importer of TV sets would have had to pay 45 per cent duty, or $225, for each set, in order to protect a mere $100 of local value that was added to the imported components—an effective duty rate of 225 per cent.

(For more on this subject, see Appendix I.)

At the time, I believed totally in the commission and in its philosophy and processes. In 1974, my colleagues and I were all true believers. The Industries Assistance Commission was an exciting place to work in, and I believed we were achieving something of great value for the Australian economy: we were dismantling an old, inefficient manufacturing-industry structure that couldn't compete internationally, and we were giving more efficient economic activities the chance to attract resources released by the demise of inefficient businesses.

(It took around 15 years for me to see the light: by about 1985, it had become obvious that the theory didn't work. We had created no new manufacturing industries. All that had been achieved was that we had put old, good manufacturers out of business; the good ones had often just moved their plants offshore. The commission's response was to drive tariff rates lower and lower. By 2009, zero was regarded as the only acceptable long-term tariff level.)

Pat Barrett, who became Australia's long-serving auditor-general, recommended my promotion to director. This was the recognised take-off point for a senior management career in the economic portfolios of the government.

I was asked if I would go to Canberra to meet Sir Peter Nixon, the chairman of the Public Service Board, and Sir Alan Westerman, the secretary of the Treasury. I did so, and we had lunch at the Commonwealth Club, where I was asked if I wanted to come to Canberra as an assistant commissioner. If I'd accepted, I would have then spent an almost obligatory two years at the World Bank.

Instead, I left the public service. This followed a bitter dispute between the presiding commissioner (Hylda Rolfe) and an associate commissioner (Stuart Cossar) who were responsible for the batteries inquiry. The chairman at the time (Bill McKinnon) joined the inquiry to vote on the side of the presiding commissioner.

Before I left, I wrote Cossar's dissenting report, which the Fraser government accepted, despite the opposition of the chairman and commissioner Rolfe.

I'd broken a fundamental rule. Within the commission, you weren't supposed to help dissenters: they were marginalised by the staff, and given no assistance in the preparation of their reports. Instead, the staff wrote the majority commission reports, and framed the recommendations to government.

The commissioners met with the staff at draft-report meetings, and usually limited their direct input to some editing and minor guidance. They may have fiddled with the recommendations slightly, but the general outcome was usually evident to everyone once the public hearings were over.

Stuart Cossar was a mentor of mine in the commission. He was a patrician, absentee farmer who raised Charolaises cattle. A member of the Tariff Board before becoming an associate commissioner at the commission, he was part of the old establishment in Canberra, and had organised my lunch with Nixon and Westerman.

I think that he was surprised and grateful that I was prepared to write his dissenting report in the batteries inquiry. He and Hylda Rolfe didn't get on. He loved women, but Hylda was a strong-minded woman. She didn't have much time for Stuart, or the old executive guard at Eveready Batteries who ate steak up the front of the factory at a table with a red tablecloth while the workers ate their sandwiches at the Laminex tables.

We visited the factory and had the red-tablecloth lunch. It was not a good way to influence Hylda. She was aghast at the production process for nine-volt bicycle batteries, which involved tying six 1.5-volt batteries together with twine, and dipping the knot in molten wax. The women workers were paid piece rates. Most of the women were older, and had burn scars on the ends of their fingers.

I wrote the dissenting report because I believed that Hylda's opposition to the industry was based on concerns that were irrelevant to the tariff rates we were considering.

Associate commissioners were appointed from industry to major inquiries such as the passenger motor-vehicle inquiry. They often wrote a dissenting report, which would always be ignored, without—as I've said—having received much help in drafting it from the commission staff.

It soon became apparent to me that such hearings were simply a cosmetic step before the government lowered tariffs and removed quotas. It would have been a lot cheaper and less disruptive for industry if successive governments had simply lowered the tariffs as Whitlam did. The hearings were really exercises in hypocrisy.

The late 1970s and early 1980s saw a partial retreat in the government's attitude, when the Hawke government forced its perspective on the commission to make it accept the need for quotas in the textiles, clothing, and footwear (TCF) and passenger motor-vehicle industries. It did this by limiting the terms of reference from the treasurer to the commission.

The Button Plans for post-1984 assistance arrangements in the passenger motor-vehicle and textiles, clothing, and footwear industries began an era of tradeable quotas, but there was a major flaw in this protective measure that led to its eventual abandonment. To my mind, it failed because the government agreed to mix tariff policy with a free-market philosophy. This created an unintended consequence of unleashing industry participants who did nothing but speculate in quotas.

Quotas were sold for fortunes, generated specifically from public-policy decisions, which were paid for by the consumer. The beneficiaries were businesses with importing histories. Some made millions of dollars — at a time when this was a lot of money — out of buying and selling quotas, in return for very little effort.

Over time, I came to the realisation that quotas should not have been saleable or transferable other than by demonstrated increases or decreases in a firm's market share. They shouldn't have been auctioned, because this created a speculative market in which successful bidders could artificially create market shortages and drive up the prices of the relevant items. Car and TCF quotas became a separate financial-services activity, in which firms did nothing but buy and sell quotas. Some smarties even worked out how to hedge and create quota derivatives.

As I was leaving the commission, Stuart said two things to me that I subsequently concluded were true. He said that Bob Hawke was a mediocre intellect and that the Tariff Board was a mediocre institution.

Stuart wanted me to become a merchant banker, and he introduced me to a few bankers who were subsequently very successful. However, I didn't want to waste the nine years of international trade and industry-policy experience I had just accumulated. I decided to become a tariff consultant instead.

Chapter Three
Life After the Commission

It was truly a shock to go out into the commercial world and have to earn a living. You didn't have to think about earning money in the public service — it just arrived. And in the private sector your point of view wasn't treated as holy writ.

Being a tariff consultant was a substantial occupation in the days when tariffs were high and the structure of the Customs tariff was very complex. Since then, tariff simplification and the general reduction in duty rates have made the occupation redundant.

I spent the first 15 years of my business career arguing for the reduction of tariffs for major importers of motor vehicles, outboard engines, generators, electrical and electronic appliances, chemicals, plastics, timber and timber products, paper, paper products, and white goods — and their trade associations. The commission continued with its manufacturing industry tariff-reduction programme until the early 1990s. In those days, I could hardly have been labelled a protectionist.

Initially, I worked as a consultant for John Dunkley, who had a successful national Customs brokerage and also consulted extensively with major companies on Customs problems. I was appointed as the national consultancy director, and was responsible for industry-policy consulting. My first major client was the Australian Timber Importers' Federation. In those days, the import timber industry was subject to a specific rate of duty of a few dollars per cubic metre. (Duty rates are, generally, expressed either as a percentage of the Customs value of the goods or as a fixed amount of dollars and cents related to a specific quantity—for example, $28 per litre of alcohol in whisky, or 8 cents per stick of cigarettes.) The Australian Timber Producers' Council, the representative body for the domestic industry, had asked for an *ad valorem* tariff of 45 per cent, compared with the then-current level of a few dollars per cubic metre.

After doing some careful research, I was able to demonstrate that the local industry didn't need tariffs to replace the protection it was already getting from duty-rates: I found that, from 1945 to 1975, 80 per cent of the industry's supply of timber had continued to be locally sourced, despite the fact that the percentage (or *ad valorem*) equivalent of the specific duty-rate had got progressively lower as the price of timber had increased.

For example, at a specific duty-rate of $1 a cubic metre and an earlier import value of $10, the duty-rate percentage (its *ad valorem* equivalent) had been 10 per cent; but when, over time, the import value rose to $20, the percentage-duty equivalent of the fixed $1 rate dropped to only 5 per cent. And yet, against what should therefore have been heightened competition from imports, the local industry had continued to enjoy a very substantial share of the market. Therefore, it was relatively easy to demonstrate that the high tariff being sought had nothing to do with protecting the local industry — the only outcome, if it had been successful, would have been to constrict the supply of timber to the downstream building industry. My argument was accepted by the commission. This first consulting project was a great success, and convinced me that I had found my business career.

Soon, though, I had a significant dispute of principle with John Dunkley. He believed that tariff consultants were similar to barristers: they took a brief and argued for their client's interests, regardless of the validity of the argument or its merit in the context of industry policy and the Australian economy.

In those days, evidence was given under oath, and the commissioners often cross-examined the witnesses in front of more than a hundred industry participants. Witnesses also had the right to make supplementary submissions rebutting evidence that had been put publicly.

My view was that I had to tell the truth; otherwise, I would destroy any integrity that I could bring to my client's argument. I thought that it was useless to argue, as the Australian Timber Producers' Council had done, for a level of assistance through the tariff that could not be justified and was totally out of step with the reformist mood of the commission.

I remember Ron Fisher, the consultant for the Printing and Allied Industries Federation of Australia, submitting evidence at a paper and paper-products inquiry. He had two submissions to make: one asked for no protection; the other asked for a very high level of protection for the same goods. He submitted them at the same time, and was sworn twice in the witness box.

This process was undoubtedly excessively legalistic, but it came in an era when public hearings were almost the equivalent of royal commissions. The inquiries were recorded by Hansard stenographers, and the submissions were treated as evidence.

The presiding commissioner, David McBride, asked Fisher how he could possibly swear that he was telling the truth, given that he was presenting two arguments that were directly opposed to each other. Wisely, Fisher didn't reply. McBride was the ex-secretary of the Electrical Trades Union, and he could be fiery in comments from the bench. I don't think the commission regarded that sort of advocacy very highly.

I told a number of major companies that I was not a journalist or a propagandist. My value to them lay in being able to marshal arguments and data to support the optimal position achievable, having regard to the general industry policy in place at the time, and the commission recommendations that would inevitably follow.

John Dunkley and I separated after about 18 months. I was free to consult on my own terms.

This personal experience illustrates what I have come to believe is the key problem in the development of industry policy. Economics is not a science, and economic analysis can be biased. Statistics can be used selectively, and arguments can be left out if they counter a preferred position. This is the domain of the technocrat. Increasingly, our industry policies are given a media spin, and a great deal of data and information on particular industries is no longer freely available. The free-market policy spin was first created by consultants 30 years ago. Since then, the spinners have been ensconced in the Productivity Commission and Treasury.

I consulted to the importers group in the Federal Chamber of Automotive Industries (FCAI) from 1976 until 1991. My first great business mentor was Doug Donaldson, who was the chairman of the FCAI and chief executive officer of LNC Industries, a public company with more than 3000 employees.

LNC had the franchises for Subaru, Volkswagen, Renault, Audi, Fiat, and Lancia, and for Honda in New South Wales and Queensland. At that time, the Japanese corporate practice was to operate in one state as a subsidiary, but to let Australian franchise-holders act as importer-distributors in the other states. Over time, they gradually took over the entire network after they had gained sufficient local knowledge and contacts.

From 1975 to 1991, passenger motor-vehicle tariff rates fell from 57.5 per cent to 15 per cent, and quotas that could be sold by the holder for $2000 a car were removed in 1990. Individuals importing a car from overseas had to buy one unit of quota before they could bring it back to Australia. At that stage, people working overseas could buy an expensive new car, drive it around for a few years, and then import the car and sell it for more than they had paid for it because of the valuation policy for used cars.

New market entrants (such as Korean car-makers) couldn't enter the market, as they didn't have any historical car-quota entitlements, and no one was about to sell them any and create a new competitor in the market. Volkswagen left the Australian car market for four years because of a disagreement with LNC Industries, who owned the quota and switched it to Subaru.

The main fear of the importers was that the government would introduce passing-on provisions similar to those for sales tax, which would mean that they would not be able to appropriate the savings as tariffs were reduced. We met to discuss those fears and the best response to them—which I thought was to ignore the issue. Had it wanted to, the commission could have made a simple recommendation for a legislative change to usher in the dreaded passing-on provision, but it didn't take any such action. The commission still seemed blind to the windfall gain it was providing to local participants in the imports supply-chain.

In this environment, as we have seen, there was no point in any importer voluntarily introducing price reductions—they would all have had to respond, if they wanted to maintain their market share, and this would only have served to reduce their profits.

By 1995, when the next inquiry was held, I think that my economic inclinations were starting to become apparent. I wasn't too sympathetic to the importers' anxiety that no passing-on provisions be recommended by the commission when it inevitably recommended further tariff reductions. They got another consultant.

The FCAI has had a difficult task to reconcile conflicts of interest between its members and, in some cases, the split agendas of its major members. Ford, General Motors-Holden, and Toyota are affiliates of the largest motor-vehicle manufacturers in the world. They import small passenger vehicles in very large numbers that are rebadged as Holdens and Fords.

It is very likely that the only thing that kept the assemblers in Australia going was the concessions provided by the Automotive Competitiveness Investment Scheme (ACIS). It is likely that they are losing money on their small-scale large-vehicle assembly operations, but are making money from imports. At some stage, when the ACIS is discontinued, I suspect that the losses they have accumulated will then be applied against profits earned from future imports, and therefore they will not have to pay tax for a number of years.

LNC was my largest client from the late 1970s to the mid-1980s. I worked on the basis of a handshake agreement with Donaldson, and was paid a percentage of any refunds of Customs duty I obtained for LNC. The company had such a lucrative import business that LNC's computer-based pricing model couldn't even accommodate the excessive profit per unit that the company was making on its imported four-wheel-drive vehicles. This was all courtesy of an officially sanctioned rort administered by Canberra free-marketeers.

THE NEW ASIAN TIGER

Let me explain. The four-wheel-drive vehicles bore Customs duty-rates of 25 per cent; so, on an imported-cost base of, say, $5000, this represented an additional cost of $1250, for a total landed cost of $6250—whereupon they were delivered by LNC to the vehicle distributor at a price of around $12,000. Amazingly, a two-wheel-drive version of the same vehicle had the same imported-cost base of $5000, but bore a much higher duty-rate of 57.5 per cent ($2875) and was subject to quota restrictions, which had a per-vehicle value of $2000, for a total landed cost of $9875 and a distributor price of $11,500. The import price paid was exactly the same, but the duty difference in favour of the four-wheel-drive vehicle—and the profit margin it provided—was enormous. There was no reason for LNC to pass the gain on to the Australian consumer. In fact, there was a good reason not to: the demand for the vehicles would have become so great that the government would have brought a swift end to that policy.

I failed to convince Donaldson to accept an offer to purchase LNC's quota of 20,000 passenger motor vehicles from a German finance company, which was prepared to lease them back annually to LNC. The offer was worth $40 million a year. Quotas were a bonanza for importers in all sorts of ways, and I knew they couldn't last.

The Hawke government also gave specific grants of many millions of dollars to Dupont (another client for many years) when they bought Fibremakers from the Lieberman family; and to Kodak, led by a young Ziggy Switkowski, who went on to become the chief executive officer of Telstra. The grants were intended to bribe companies into accepting tariff reductions and the end of quotas. There were no onerous conditions imposed on the grants—just a nod and a wink that the company would not make a fuss when the quotas and high tariffs were eliminated. The recipients played their part, and didn't protest or move too quickly.

These were ad hoc donations of public monies, undertaken with the good intention of keeping the industries in Australia. The idea was to substitute a one-off payment for years of assistance. Instead, the companies took the money and ran. They viewed the government's largesse as a short-term windfall, and didn't feel under any compulsion to stay in Australia after the money had been received. After an indecent interval of only a few years, the companies made their own decisions about their local manufacturing/imports mix.

The success of my consultancy created the opportunity for me to get involved in all the day-to-day functions of Customs, storage, and cartage. I started a Customs agency, a container-carrying company, and a Customs bond store, and set up an empty container depot on land rented from ICI. The glossary explains what these businesses did. They are all part of the cross-border logistics and compliance-service chain that most large importers now use, rather than in-house providers.

At the time, Port Botany was just starting to replace Darling Harbour and the old Walsh Bay, White Bay, and Woolloomooloo wharves in Sydney Harbour as the major port for container vessels. We moved our business to a five-acre site at Port Botany in 1981, to a building that was a ruined salt warehouse, filled with seagull droppings. The business behind us was ICI, the English chemical plant. Believe it or not, the creek between us and ICI often caught fire.

This business expansion led me to gain a level of practical knowledge about importing and exporting logistics and compliance processes that simply wasn't available in the rarefied atmosphere of industry-policy consultancy. Logistics was an unknown term in those days, but the growth of container imports and exports was phenomenal. It was easy to convince our happy clients that we could do just as good a job with their importing costs as we had with their submissions to government and to Customs.

In particular, we created a reputation for separating the cost elements in import shipments that were to be used for Customs valuation purposes. Our philosophy was that importers should only pay duty on the value of the imported goods themselves; that was what the duty was intended to protect. Importers shouldn't have to pay duty on overseas transport of the goods, port storage, documentation, buying agents' commissions, or interest charges for delayed payment. The tariffs were about protection against overseas manufactured products, not against services and charges incidental to the movement of the goods.

When we started the refund audits, the valuation legislation comprised two paragraphs in the Customs Act. By the time we finished, the legislation on valuation in the Customs Act was 23 pages long. For seven years, we were the largest Customs refund-lodgers in Australia.

Then, in 1986, I was approached to join Deloitte because their deputy chairman was on the board of LNC Industries and Monier. He wanted to create a joint venture between our consulting company and Deloitte. He was aware of the dollar value of our service to importers.

I accepted the offer. I had lost money in the practical world of container carrying and warehouse operation, mainly through being the meat in the sandwich between the Waterside Workers Federation, the Storemen and Packers Union, and the Transport Workers Union in a meaningless demarcation dispute aimed at having a single union operate in the deconsolidated depots at Port Botany. Only three depots were approved by the trade union junta to pack and unpack containers of goods for more than one consigner. We were declared black by the unions, and for 18 months couldn't use the warehouse we had built. We also had 13 idle semi-trailers. Our applications to the Industrial Tribunal for relief always went nowhere.

I also thought that the first-tier accounting and legal firms would eventually squeeze out boutique Customs consultancies like mine. (As it turned out, they never did, because they lacked the empirical knowledge so critical to operating successfully in the logistics and Customs-compliance industry.)

Our joint venture with Deloitte ended in 1991 when Deloitte merged with Touche Ross and Tohmatsu (the largest auditing firm in Japan). The international firms didn't want exotic business arrangements in a number of countries. They wanted to deliver a single message.

In 1991, I became the partner in charge of business taxes (Customs duty, sales tax, payroll tax, and transfer pricing) at Deloitte, Haskins and Sells (subsequently Deloitte, Ross Tohmatsu, and now simply Deloitte).

Then, in 1992, I was head hunted, along with 12 of my staff: I became a partner in Ernst & Young, with national responsibility for transfer pricing, Customs, and industry policy. I also became the New South Wales leader of the manufacturing industry group within Ernst & Young.

I spent seven years as the partner nationally responsible for international trade, Customs compliance, and transfer pricing in Deloitte and then Ernst & Young. By 1990, refunds of Customs duty had become of little interest to large importers because duty rates were so low. Luckily, transfer pricing was the next big international tax problem for multinational companies. It remains a major taxation-compliance problem to the present time.

In 1994, Adrian Firmstone and I left Ernst & Young to establish our own boutique legal and indirect-tax practice. We left because it was obvious that we could make a lot more money working for the clients that we had brought to the major accounting firms of Deloitte and Ernst & Young than by working for them within those practices. There were simply too many meetings, too many unprofitable interstate responsibilities, and too many politicians to deal with. We took with us one partner, Kevin O'Rourke, who has since become a partner in PricewaterhouseCoopers, and two senior managers who also became partners in our firm and later moved on to major legal firms as partners. A number of our staff also came with us.

Adrian had been a taxation officer, a partner in KPMG, and the partner nationally responsible for sales tax and indirect taxes at Ernst & Young. He was simply the best sales tax consultant in Australia.

Our clients included Woolworths, Coles, Coca Cola, ACI, Harvey Norman, the Australian Hotels Association, Clubs NSW, Dick Smith, Dupont, car importers, components manufacturers, Crown Forklifts, Louis Vuitton, the Australian Taxation Office, David Jones, Eli Lilly, Chevron, cosmetics companies, and Strathfield Car Radio. We were involved in a lot of litigation, and ended up in the High Court a few times, contesting decisions made by either Customs or the Australian Taxation Office.

This business relationship ended with Adrian's premature

death in 2006. He was a brilliant man who loved life. We proved that you didn't have to be a first-tier firm to compete in the exotic areas of indirect tax, Customs, and transfer pricing.

I suppose that the most important lesson I have drawn from 30 years' experience of business consultancy and the provision of physical logistics concerns the great difference between theory and practice.

If I had never left the public service, I would have missed the opportunity to learn and understand that the economy and the market do not follow dominant theories and set textbooks. Economists, like historians, are prisoners of their time, their place, their prejudices, and their environment.

When I began my consultancy career, I believed that the quality of the industry and economic analysis that I provided was everything. I was successful, and worked for a lot of large clients in major industries. But, as time went by, I could see that some clients were happy to retain relationships with service providers who delivered only good, average-quality work, but no more, and often wondered why. I came to realise that the main reason was simply that, for most clients, 'good is good enough'. Importers involved in cross-border matters such as transfer pricing, dumping, and the technicality of Customs classification and valuation normally lack the knowledge to understand the difference between good and excellent work. They recognise bad work much more readily, because it often fails to even partially achieve its purpose.

If the work is good, it usually takes an adverse management change to lose a client. New owners or senior managers often have their own team of advisers.

The major lesson I learned in business was that personal relationships are paramount so long as the quality of the work is good. I think that this is about trusting the external consultant, and being able to initiate a quick and effective response to government policy or trade issues that emerge. Most chief executives make a lot of decisions each day across a wide range of competencies and issues. The best of them delegate to trusted confederates.

Track records are powerful assets for any service provider. Again, they demonstrate the commercial value of empirical performance over academic analysis.

Chapter Four
My Own Seismic Shift

A seismic shift usually concerns movements in the earth's tectonic plates that cause earthquakes. The development of those changes take a very long time, but the ultimate outcome is of huge and devastating proportions.

Throughout the 1980s, I had accepted the conventional wisdom of the Industries Commission with growing disquiet. In the motor-vehicle, timber, chemicals, and plastics industries, we had made submissions to the commission that proved central to the outcomes. I had told my clients that they needed to spend time and money to ensure that they were major players in the inquiries and in influencing the government's ultimate decisions.

This perspective ignored the fact that the recommendations of the commission were set in stone before each inquiry began. There was virtually no wiggle room, even on relatively minor issues. In each inquiry, the commission calculated the dollar value of tariff-reduction benefits that it was purportedly handing to the consumer. I knew that these amounts were risible — movements in exchange rates, the absence of legislation requiring the passing on of the duty reductions, and the lack of market advantage for any first mover reducing prices meant that the exporters, the importers, or the retailers would always keep the duty reductions as a windfall gain. My clients could have saved their money, kept away, and let the commission do its work unaided, and they would have achieved the same result.

Every major country was reducing tariffs in the 1980s, but every country except Australia was introducing non-tariff forms of assistance to their manufacturers that usually more than compensated for the tariff loss. Australia was the global virgin. We removed state government preferences, two ex-chairmen (Rattigan and his successor) of the commission wrote a book advocating the merits of unilateral tariff protection and condemning the countries that were 'backsliders', and any form of non-tariff protection was eradicated.

My ultimate outing as an advocate for Australian manufacturing took over ten years, and cost me a lot of clients and a few friends. I wasn't too concerned because I could see that the subject of transfer pricing was turning into a major new market for me. Lower tariffs meant that importers didn't need to display the same level of interest in restructuring their import values to ensure that they were only paying the duty that they had to pay. Finally, the industry-review programme was, essentially, finished. Motor cars, and textiles, clothing, and footwear were the only industries with tariffs higher than the general industry rate.

It wasn't a simple, pragmatic shift of my position. The manufacturers were scarcely likely to embrace me, as I had worked for major importers for too long for them to believe that I could passionately present their interests. The core of the commission's philosophy had been to create a brave new world of outward looking, internationally competitive manufacturers. As we have seen, the mechanism to do this was founded in the belief that resources released by the removal of tariff distortions would flow to more efficient industries. There was no reason, in its view, why these industries had to be manufacturers. The idea of neutral resource-allocation was the beginning of the major push for deregulation and the end of government intervention in the market. It sounded good, but it was a lot of codswallop then—and still is now. All that happened was that importers increased their share of the Australian market, our manufacturers' market-share shrank, and our current-account deficits and foreign debt continued to pile up at an ever-increasing rate.

My official exit from the protectionist closet came after prime minister Paul Keating's economic statement in 1992, when he declared the tariff debate 'dead'. By then, I had been appointed the national leader of Deloitte's manufacturing industry group, and I used the occasion of the keynote address I gave on Keating's statement at a dinner hosted by the Committee for Economic Development of Australia to come out. (Other speakers included true believers Dr Chris Caton, chief economist at Bankers Trust; Professor Barry Hughes, Keating's adviser when he was treasurer; and journalist Paddy McGuinness.)

To begin with, I quoted Scipio Africanus, the conqueror of Carthage, who had threatened Rome's destruction through the brilliance of the Carthaginian general, Hannibal: 'Scipio Africanus always began a speech by saying that Carthage must be destroyed. I intend to start all future speeches by saying that Australia has to reduce its current-account deficit.'

I kept that promise reasonably faithfully for the next 15 years.

I had earlier signalled my shift to the other side of the debate. On 11 June 1991, the *Australian Financial Review* had published an article of mine titled 'Buzz Words Cluttering Industrial Vision,' which included these comments:

> We live in an age of seductive buzzwords and buzz theories. Words such as free, open, international, competitive, and phrases such as outward looking and level playing field are powerful tools in the hands of the theorists who have succeeded in almost eliminating any coherent policy of assistance to Australian manufacturing industry.
>
> The rhetoric and the strategy have not been realised. Australia's commitment to resource allocation theory has not thrown up those competitive industries it was supposed to promote. The tariff reduction programme did not create internationally competitive, outward-looking exporting manufacturing industries. It was irrelevant to that goal. In short, we need to grow up in our trade strategy. It is scandalous that our government policy should be led by naïve theories that flowed from the British economists of the 19th century.

This was the only article I've written that the *Australian Financial Review* has ever published.

Few companies caught up in the industry-review programme ever understood that the specific commission inquiry to which they made submissions or gave evidence wasn't really about them. The government's policy had to be designed to benefit all the participants in the industry — not just one company. Ultimately, the policy had to be of benefit to the Australian economy. This was the unarguable concept in its pure form, but no one ever reviewed the banks, the doctors, the lawyers, the finance sector, the insurance companies, or any of the other industry groups that had received special assistance from state governments and federal governments over the previous century.

The trouble was that the econometric models created by the academics didn't reflect market reality and were not dynamic. They ignored the possibility that resources released by the industries closed down would lie idle rather than flow to the most efficient and financially attractive alternative use. They ignored the possibility of change. Finally, they ignored the fact that most people were not prepared to engage in a constant process of re-education and migration to move to new jobs in new places.

But there was no way that this could be sensibly discussed. If you weren't a true believer in the neo-classical theory, you were marginalised. You had to believe in the power of the market.

By 1996, Keating had finished the tariff-demolition job that had been started by Gough Whitlam and moved along by Bob Hawke. Malcolm Fraser had not shown the zeal for tariff reform of Gough Whitlam; though, during the Fraser years, the Industries Commission continued its manufacturing review, focusing on the benchmark tariff of 25 per cent.

Keating had also radically altered the Australian economy by setting in motion a revolution that was to sweep away old values such as full-time employment at a company for most of your life, paying off your home over 25 years, and retiring on the pension.

Some people would say that this was a good thing. It certainly created an Australian version of the Russian oligarchy who grew rich on their government connections and consultancies, public-private partnerships, and stock-market touting. It also created the so-called New Economy.

The New Economy promoted the belief that financial success had little to do with hard work and application. In 1994, the information-technology revolution was just arriving, and the 'tech wreck' or dot-com bust of 2001 (which was to cost the world US$3 trillion) was far away. Everyone could be a winning player in the share market, and would work in the services sector. Banks got rid of bank managers, and introduced their alienated customers to financial planners who received most of their income from commissions on financial products. Poker machines were introduced into hotels (except in Western Australia), which certainly revitalised that industry.

The New Economy was to be driven by the services sector. It would replace the rust belt of old and unfashionable manufacturing factories. This shift was vital, we were told, if we were to maintain our standard of living.

Productivity improvements were supposed to take care of the declining manufacturing sector. This was an old-economy industry. We could do a lot more with less of it, or else buy in its products from China. Manufacturing and agriculture were tolerated only because no one had yet figured out how to eat and wear share certificates.

The only variable in the equation that was missing was a method of re-educating and employing the great mass of the Australian population in the services sector, and getting them to make their superannuation payments. This was largely solved by encouraging women to rejoin the workforce, making two-income families the norm, and generating a massive number of part-time, low-paid, and unprotected jobs in the services sector.

Our much-vaunted full employment (which was, in turn, dependent on full-time employment being attributed to anyone who was employed for at least one hour a week) came from the retailers' shelf-packers, the check-out operators, the students emptying poker machines and pouring beers in hotels and clubs, the TAB and Tabcorp outlets, the call-centre workers (before they were offshored), and the burgeoning aged-care industry. Australia had invented its own 'Mexican' class of casual and poorly paid workers, which has its parallel in the illegal immigrant servant class of California and Texas.

The retail and health and aged-care sectors currently employ nearly a quarter of the Australian workforce. Another 11 per cent are employed in the logistics industry. This is the industry that transports, stores, packs, and unpacks consumer goods. Manufacturing now employs less than 10 per cent of the Australian workforce.

Close to two million people are underemployed in the Australian workforce of 12 million (according to a Bureau of Statistics report of May 2009, the figure is 13.5 per cent, without taking into account such factors as reduced hours in the hotel industry). No one has mentioned the waste of time involved in these people travelling to and from split shifts, or in turning up for shifts that last two hours. They often spend more time going to and from work by spasmodic late-night public transport than working.

There is no doubt that, in the past 30 years, we have created an underclass in Australia that is alienated from the mainstream of our society. The first in that group are our oldest citizens: indigenous Australians. Many of them are still living in camps outside country towns or in traditionally poor suburbs such as Sydney's Redfern. Nearly half their children have ear infections that render them partially deaf. How can you learn at school when you can't hear?

The balance of the people in our city underclass live in caravan parks, government housing, units and flats, and suburbs far removed from the city centres, or in inner-city ghettos. Often casual workers, they may be from the Pacific islands, New Zealand, or from African states that are constantly involved in civil wars.

There is also an ever-increasing number of international students who work to pay the rent and to feed themselves. Their parents struggle to pay the fees, and the students must support themselves.

In rural Australia, the poor live in virtually abandoned

small towns, in caravan parks, and in houses left deserted after a farm was sold and consolidated into a larger holding.

Finally, many of our young (and not so young) people live with their parents. They are underemployed, and can't afford to leave home.

Over the last 20 years, the media has had a lot to answer for. Commentators praised the New Economy, and denigrated the old values. They contributed to the marginalisation of any dissenters. Most of the media were dazzled by the new generation of financial spivs and closed-minded academics; some still are. None of the new economists were interested in research and analysis. The media didn't allocate enough time for investigative journalism — which, though perhaps boring, was crucial for the economy.

Some journalists — such as Tim Colebatch, Ken Davidson, Michael Short, Brian Toohey, and Lincoln Wright — maintained their journalistic integrity. A lot didn't.

Australian manufacturers were very gun shy, and certainly didn't confront the Keating government. They didn't get any consideration from the Howard government either, unless they were a big multinational business or one of the few Australian billionaires. The Howard government was a true believer in the ascendancy of the New Economy, in which the services sector was dominant.

But there were some who did oppose the triumphant march of free-market economics and the annihilation of the Australian manufacturing sector. The first dissenter in the press was economist Dr Bill Weekes, who expressed his reservations, first in the Melbourne *Herald* in the late 1980s, and then in more than fifty articles in *The Age*.

Bill was also the managing director of Onkaparinga, the

iconic Australian woollen blanket company. He proved that high quality, high-value-added Australian woollen products could be exported to the rest of the world.

With businessmen Ernest Rodeck and John Siddons, Bill founded the Society for Balanced Trade. Its driving philosophy was to try to achieve a reasonable balance over time between the income we earned from exports and what we paid for imports. It was as simple as that.

Former Victorian premier Sir Rupert (Dick) Hamer was the society's patron. Hamer attended virtually all our meetings in a neat, plain business suit that revealed he hadn't got much out of the perks of office. He was a patron who rolled up his sleeves, engaged in the debate, and gave a lot more to the society than his name until his death in 2004.

Ernest Rodeck was a senior executive and board member of a number of major Australian companies. His first success was to create Fler Furniture (whose name derived from the initial letters of the first names of its co-founders, Fred Lowen and Ernest Rodeck) and to float it on the Australian Stock Exchange. Ernest has worked for the society with a relentless passion that, in most people, has usually diminished by the time we turn seventy. He was still involved at the age of ninety.

John Siddons was the son of the founder of Siddons, a major tool-manufacturing company, and deputy leader of the Australian Democrats. John worked hard for the society, and has never lost interest in its cause.

There is a long roll-call of people who had the courage to stand against the flow and question the direction that the economy was taking. They include Sid Spindler, a Democrat senator, who was on the committee for years; Billy Wentworth, a long-standing member of parliament, was still arguing for the cause well into his nineties; and entrepreneur Derek Sicklen, who contributed $250,000 of his own money. Bob Santamaria, founder of the National Civic Council, argued our case; and Evan Jones, an academic from Sydney University, blighted his career by refusing to join what was the populist academic push of free-market economics.

John Legge, Robert Manne, John Carroll, Gregory Clarke, James Fox, Neil Walford, and Frank Stillwell were also early dissidents. Kerry Packer was also a sceptic.

The only union leader who had the guts to stand up for industry was Doug Cameron of the Australian Workers' Union. The other trade union leaders were more interested in demarcation issues, collecting dues, and advancing their own careers. In all the manufacturing-industry hearings I attended, both as a staffer and as a consultant appearing before the commission, the unions never once mounted a strong defence of their industry. They took their cue from Bob Hawke, Paul Keating, and Bill Kelty, who disappeared in a huff when Keating lost. Long after Keating was gone, the ACTU genuflected to his ideas.

This is not a complete list of the people who were prepared to be marginalised and ridiculed because they disagreed with what quickly became the conventional wisdom on both sides of politics and in all parts of the media. I am sorry if I have missed you — you deserve at least one footnote for your stoic courage in the face of what was usually abuse rather than refutation.

Since 1992, John Spooner and I have teamed to illustrate and write more than 80 articles for *The Age* discussing the many consequences and policies of what has been variously called economic rationalism, neo-liberalism, and free-market economics. Ernie Sharkey was a great editor and proof-reader for many articles.

In that time, we have watched Australia's foreign debt grow from $218 billion to $700 billion. We have seen Australian manufacturing's proportion of national income cut to less than half its 1972 level, and the annihilation of employment and knowledge in great industries. For 30 years, Australians have lived beyond their means. Imports have always exceeded exports, even during the brief iron-and-coal export bubble of 2008, when services are taken into account.

We have the 12th-largest foreign debt in the world, but we are not the 12th-largest country. We have the fourth-highest current-account deficit of 189 countries listed by the US's Central Intelligence Agency. Some of the countries down the bottom with us are there because they are the home countries of the great multinational firms, and their wealth is scattered throughout the planet. We are not in that circumstance.

Some of us cried out that this situation shouldn't exist or continue in a nation as rich as ours. For our pains, we were mocked and marginalised by the economic establishment.

There were half-hearted warnings from parts of the establishment. In April 2001, Glen Stevens, now governor but then assistant governor (economic) of the Reserve Bank of Australia, said in a speech to the Melbourne Institute's Business Economic Forum: 'At some stage surely this pace of debt accumulation will lessen ... for a start we will probably see a return to somewhat higher rates of current savings.'

It got worse, not better. The banks did nothing to encourage savings. I'm glad that, apart from interest rates, the RBA isn't in the economic-forecasting business.

We are now embroiled in a global financial disaster that

will cost the world tens of trillions of dollars, destroy great companies, and create a level of unemployment that has not been seen since the Great Depression of the 1930s.

Personal losses that were unknown in the 1930s are now occurring. People are losing a substantial part of their superannuation; and their other major asset, their home, is decreasing in value. Two of the great advances of the second half of the twentieth century in Australia provided ordinary people with the apparent security of being able, eventually, to own their own home and then being able to save to retire and maintain their standard of living in their old age. That mirage is dissolving.

It turns out that we have lived beyond our means for a very long time.

***

Our current-account deficit crisis and our foreign debt are a direct consequence of the economic-policy path that we have single-mindedly pursued for the past 35 years. This path has been consciously chosen by the main economic advisers to successive governments, supported by modelling techniques that were developed during that period.

The ultimate aim of this book is to tell you how we got into the economic mess that we are presently in, and to suggest some ways out of it. My starting point is that economic theories and econometric modelling are interesting and valuable concepts and methodologies, but they often have little direct relevance and value in our economy. They are based on too many false assumptions to enable a direct correlation to be made with the complex processes that actually take place in the economy. They need to be treated with a great deal of caution.

The popularity of economic models is a lot like magic. The audience doesn't know how it is done, but sees a result. By the time someone works out the simple illusion, the magician has moved on to the next trick. Future projects, such as the economists' view that the mineral boom would last indefinitely, can simply be forgotten in the flush of the next set of projections. The trouble is that something always happens in the future that we haven't counted on — you can certainly count on that. But most people never match up past predictions with present events.

One obvious systemic error is that virtually all economic models are static. They do not take into account the constant flow of change in an industry, a sector, or an economy. They do not include the lags that are always present in any economic activity. Almost the greatest business lesson you can learn is that any new product or process takes twice as long to be productive and bring to market, and costs twice as much to make, as you expected it to. Invention is not as important as dissemination in the market.

Generally, we do not second-guess lawyers, doctors, accountants, engineers, or any other owner of specialised knowledge. These people are 'professionals', and we expect them to be correct in their field of knowledge. Lawyers work on precedents, and doctors work with a body of case studies, and massive research and funding by pharmaceutical companies. Accountants have generally accepted accounting principles, and libraries of taxation rulings. Engineers have major analyses of stress and building standards.

Economists have their imaginations, some rudimentary understanding of mathematics (compared to a pure mathematician or a nuclear physicist), and some jargon. Economics is a soft science. It does not examine, calculate outcomes, and employ the empirical evidence that other professions use to support their advice. Economics does not base its theorems or projections upon the evolution and refinement of ideas through observation.

Beyond manufacturing, there has been a lot of protection and government assistance provided to the banking, insurance, and finance industries, as well as the professions, over the last 50 years. But no one seems to have been concerned about eliminating or even commenting on these barriers to imported services.

This is, to a large extent, a monumental piece of self-serving hypocrisy. Most participants in those industries and professions have been advocates of the free market—except where it impacts on them. Multinational companies are ruthless protectors of their brand names and intellectual property. The World Trade Organisation Agreement Treaty for the Protection of Intellectual Property Rights (TRIPS) requires the compulsory commitment of member countries. TRIPS has allowed multinational companies to insist that police in foreign jurisdictions seize and destroy fake products bearing their name or made in the image of their products. Foreign courts must also consider legal cases brought against any infringement.

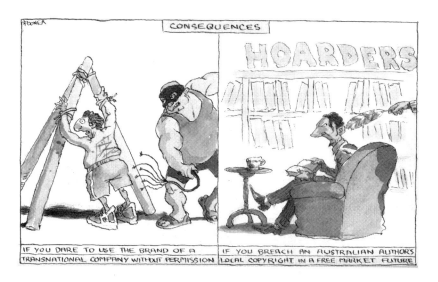

Patent protection has prevented the free flow of many major pharmaceuticals to developing countries. All of these drugs can be reverse engineered, but doing so will bring massive retaliation down on those who do so and on the countries in which they are located.

There is a strong argument that this sort of protection is necessary if firms are to be encouraged to make an investment in research and development to invent and disseminate new products. But why is this any different to the manufacturing-assistance argument?

***

After decades of having contributed to and observed tariff-reduction programmes, I've come to a major empirical observation: tariffs don't mean much anymore in Australia. There is still some angst within the Productivity Commission about our current 5 per cent tariff, but in my view this level is meaningless. There are even lots of ways for importers to obtain tariff concessions that reduce duty-rates to zero. Freight costs, financial costs, Customs-clearance costs, transport costs, and every other cross-border cost were substantially reduced over the 30 years from 1975 to 2005. In most countries — but not in Australia — they were replaced by more onerous non-tariff barriers.

The costs associated with the physical movement of good from overseas to Australia have also declined while those costs have been increasing in other countries. For example, many of the homeland security measures implemented at the US border following the September 11 attacks have created non-tariff barriers for exporters to the United States.

We have come from tariff equivalents of over 100 per cent — and even if these rates still existed, they would be nowhere near enough to protect a domestic textiles, clothing, and footwear industry from imports manufactured in India, Indonesia, or China.

To create government policies designed to encourage a local manufacturing industry, other forms of industry assistance are needed. Tariffs were an old barrier to trade; but, in most industries, they stopped working in the 1970s. The passenger motor-vehicle and textiles, clothing, and footwear industries had meaningful tariff protection up until 1990, but quotas were more powerful measures. The United States and the European Union found that using quotas in one form or another (including voluntary restraints and temporary quotas) was the only way to stop the annihilation of their own manufacturing industries.

The high point of Australian motor-vehicle manufacturing came during the Button 80:20 market-sharing plan, when the level of vehicle imports was less than 10 per cent. Today, imports supply about 80 per cent of the market, and even this number doesn't fully reflect the devastation that has been wreaked in the components industry. The car assemblers now use world prices for components, and will import any component that is not priced at the global level. In 2010, it is likely that Ford will cease making the Ford Falcon. Preliminary estimates of local manufacturing suggest that the industry will make (or assemble from a mix of local and imported components) the lowest number of cars produced since 1957.

The Australian Bureau of Statistics used to publish annual Year Books, which contained statistics of imports sorted by quantity and value, county of origin, tariff concessions, and statistical codes. These publications provided a great deal of information that allowed anyone interested to be completely up to date with the state of import-penetration in their industry. Confidentiality was provided in circumstances where companies would otherwise be able to directly identify the business transactions of their competitors.

This publication no longer exists, for reasons best known to government.

The value of such statistics can be shown by a present-day example in the passenger motor-vehicle industry. In 2006, the number of passenger motor vehicles manufactured in Australia had fallen to 200,000 units in a market of one million units — that is, we were only supplying 20 per cent of the market. As little as 18 months before, we were supplying 300,000 units. In 1985, we were manufacturing 600,000 units in a market of less than 700,000 motor vehicles.

Australia ranks about 20th amongst the world's passenger motor-vehicle manufacturers. The other 19 countries all increased their production of passenger motor vehicles over the 21-year period from 1985 to 2006. We are the only country that declined over that period.

AN ECONOMISTS IDEA OF WHERE CARS COME FROM

We only manufacture large and medium-sized vehicles; in fact, we produce over 99 per cent of the large vehicles sold in Australia. The manufacturers in Australia are Ford, General

Motors, and Toyota. They are the largest global manufacturers in the world, and obviously have decided to manufacture small, environmentally friendly, fuel-efficient vehicles in places other than Australia.

This started to change in 2009, thanks to government subsidies of some billions of dollars for a green-car production programme, and to the belated recognition by global car manufacturers that people no longer want large fuel-guzzlers. The government's plan has been strenuously opposed by free-market economists.

The passenger motor-vehicle industry and its Australian component suppliers employed 160,000 people in 1985. That number has probably now halved to about 80,000. It is still an industry that is the core of our light-engineering and production-process skills and innovation.

Tragically, the solution to the decline in local vehicle manufacture, the shrinkage of employment in the industry, and the loss of one of the core contributors to our industry engineering skills was readily to be found in the measures imposed in other countries — many with a smaller domestic market than Australia — that have convinced the major global manufacturers to establish small-vehicle production lines there. They lowered tariffs, like we did, but substituted non-tariff barriers that worked.

The most successful piece of government and media propaganda in the manufacturing-industry policy debate is the continuous assertion that eliminating high tariffs has made consumer goods cheaper. In fact, given that the mark-up between the landed duty-paid price of a good and its retail price is often some hundreds of per cent, duty-rate reductions of even 20 per cent of the Customs value have never mattered much. The truth is that the prices of many consumer durables such as TVs, refrigerators, and cars have been lowered significantly because of production innovations and the concentration of global manufacturing plants in low-cost countries with poor environmental and labour regulations.

Tariffs, based on import Customs valuations, were always irrelevant to such developments, except when they were increased and an excuse was thereby created for all importers to raise their prices across the entire market. Price reductions have occurred in the last twenty years because exporters and importers have become competitive against each other rather than local manufacturers. In the 1990s, Korean car imports were cheaper than Japanese car imports, and captured part of the Australian market precisely because of their price advantage. By the mid-1990s, it was obvious to me (and anyone who was prepared to look) that car prices hadn't fallen after tariff reductions and the removal of quotas. By then I was persona non grata with the Federal Chamber of Automotive Industries and the car importers. As we have seen, the latter had been terrified at the 1991 inquiry (when I represented them) that they would be forced to pass on the inevitable tariff reductions.

***

My second empirical observation is that multinational companies often make more after-tax profit out of intellectual property and tax avoidance than out of making global products. This is not a jaundiced view. In May 2009, President Obama nominated the top 100 American corporations as targets for a review by the US's Internal Revenue Service. He stated that they paid $17 billion in tax on profits of $700 billion, or less than 3 per cent. They obviously didn't make or take their profits in the United States.

The obsolete multinational view is that you manufacture at home or in countries that provide either tax breaks or cheap labour. But the idea of manufacturing at home is now disappearing. China and India provide very cheap labour, as well as lax environmental restrictions. They are cheaper than Turkey, Malaysia, and Indonesia, which were favourite locations for a few years, and they have no unions and no worker protection.

The major profit really lies in the payments made by manufacturing subsidiaries for intellectual property, the licensing of brand names, and the application of manufacturing know-how, and a host of other intangible payments. Loans are often made to the affiliates to keep them viable.

In the new global manufacturing model, Chinese, Indian, and other environmentally indifferent countries offer low labour costs, and manufacturers receive a very low price for the goods.

Multinationals have used a range of tax havens and countries with primitive taxation regimes to install entities owning their intangible and intellectual properties. It is extremely difficult for taxation authorities to trace where payments for these properties have ended up. Double-tax treaties (which are agreements as to the rate of withholding tax that both countries impose on payments made overseas for interest on loans and royalty payments) have been signed by 150 countries, and they also provide an incentive for manufacturers to focus on building a global brand name and associated intellectual property. It is a lot more tax effective to sell intellectual property than to shift physical goods from one market to the other: tax rates in the double-tax treaties are commonly half the company tax rates applying in a foreign jurisdiction.

Transfer pricing is discussed in detail elsewhere in this book. At this point, it is important to understand that transfer pricing is not just about avoiding, reducing, or delaying tax payments in the simple sense. The ability to pay little tax also creates a massive competitive advantage for multinationals in terms of their cashflows. Australia has always been a good environment for small and medium-sized business, but that is fading fast because our manufacturers can't compete with multinational imports. Those imports aren't subject to significant duties, and a major part of the profit on sales doesn't occur in Australia either, or is delayed—allowing the affiliate or parent company to use the money for years.

Creative, talented accountants can defer income, dividends, and profits for a very long time through all sorts of provisions, including the supply of additional working capital. Income can sit in an affiliate's books and be a considerable asset long before it is brought to account for taxation purposes. Loans and charges between affiliates and a parent company can also sit in the books for years. Their disclosure is usually enough to satisfy the taxation authorities—the authorities don't try to tell the companies how to treat working capital or inter-company debts, or when to bring them to finality.

No one has ever investigated the length of time that multinationals defer taking up their nett obligations from cross-border transactions. Access to cross-border financial deals without any external pressure for final settlements of accounts is itself a major business advantage.

***

My conversion to the idea that we have to look after our own came about because it eventually became obvious to me that we were selling off our land, our businesses, our property, and our resources to sustain a services sector that produced nothing tangible, and to buy imports that replaced local manufactures by borrowing from overseas.

There has been no concerted and overarching analysis of manufacturing industry in our economy for 20 years. Except for prosecuting the last of the motor-vehicle and textiles, clothing, and footwear tariff wars, the Productivity Commission stopped reviewing manufacturing industry at the end of the 1980s. The Australian Bureau of Statistics has stopped its historical industry reviews.

No one can tell us how much of our nation and our economy we still own, and the government certainly doesn't want to. I think it is less than 50 per cent. This is not sustainable, either for our sovereignty or our well-being.

THE ELEPHANT ON THE ROOM

Chapter Five
Free-Market Australia

In 1991, Paul Keating finally got the numbers to overthrow Australia's great populist, Bob Hawke, to become prime minister. In his February 1992 Economic Statement, during which he announced that 'the tariff debate is dead', Keating declared that he 'was bringing to an end our sorry involvement with protection'. His major goal was to reconstruct and open up the Australian economy.

Deregulation, microeconomic reform, and outward-looking, externally oriented, internationally competitive service-sector industries were the toys that Keating got out of the cupboard to create his reputation as the great reformer.

The problem was that he didn't know enough about the subjects and wouldn't listen to anyone other than the acolytes whom he chose as advisers. You didn't work for Paul unless you were a true believer in Paul's greatness. He was the great Marginaliser.

Paul Keating had little regard for the public service. He began what has become a continuing tradition of employing like-minded or subservient advisers, and ignoring the public service (except for those who tap the mat when they are used to put a Westminster-style gloss on a politically expedient outcome).

He replaced his permanent head, Tony Cole, who had been the chairman of the Industries Commission. That sent the appropriate message to any departmental secretaries who thought they might retain their political neutrality.

Keating's vision for Australia is often lauded. I don't believe in the cult of the individual, and Keating worship was certainly that. Keating was good looking, had style, looked well decked out in a black suit, and employed a great line of invective — but he suffered badly from a combination of his own hubris and ignorance.

A lot of the bile sounded funny, but it wasn't really appropriate. Many of the insults were simply old working-class expressions such as, 'They couldn't raffle a chook in a pub' (the opposition), or, 'It's like being flogged with a warm lettuce' (responding to criticism from the opposition leader, John Hewson).

Keating and his staff didn't bother to read Ministerials, which are briefing papers that are expressly meant to be read by the minister. They are the conduit between senior public-servant experts in particular policy areas and the ministers. This was an incredible attitude to adopt, given the ambit and complexity of policy, and the in-depth knowledge of some public servants, many of whom had spent decades developing a policy specialisation.

From Keating onwards, public servants have lost their independence. At senior levels, they now work to find solutions and policy justifications for the party that is in power. We now have a 'spoils system', whereby the new government can and does change heads of departments, and the minister's advisers are often policy-makers.

The Rudd government originally made a point of not changing too many departmental heads, but I still think that a lot of the power has moved to the advisers, who are political careerists in their own right and have often been leaders of the younger group in the political party. The advisers often have very little understanding of particular policy issues, but are part of a new guard moving through what is really a political career structure. They are keen to intervene and second-guess the public servants.

The exception would be Treasury, where the secretary, Ken Henry, has developed a public personality. I believe that the Labor government is frightened of Treasury.

Hawke had focused on the prices and income accord with the Australian Council of Trade Unions, and had given the minister of industry and commerce, John Button, his head in motor vehicles and in textiles, clothing, and footwear to establish very high tariff and quota barriers in his industry plans. The plans were very interventionist, and tried to create production-scale economies and to limit the proliferation of short production-runs. Hawke had no animus towards manufacturing industry; but he was content to let others, including Keating, run the free-market agenda.

As Keating's star rose, Button's plans became increasingly unstable. The rorts of the quota trade didn't help. By 1990, the idea of industry plans was no longer a viable policy option.

By this time, it was evident to me that the industry plans had either been rorted or hadn't fulfilled the government's goals. The plans either gave the industry public money (as with BHP, Fibremakers, and Kodak) or gave them quantitative import restrictions (in the motor-vehicles, and textiles, clothing, and footwear industries). John Button had never had factional support in the Labor Party, and his plans had provided a windfall gain to, mostly, the big end of town. They took the money and continued to reduce their manufacturing and their labour forces. The intention of the Button plans had been to create more efficient and internationally competitive industries, but it simply didn't happen.

Keating was the real architect of free-market economics in Australia. In this, Australia followed the lead of the US president, Ronald Reagan, and Britain's prime minister, Margaret Thatcher. The implosion of the Soviet Union and its satellites, the reunification of Germany, and the bankruptcy of Mexico and Argentina occurred either during Keating's long tenure as treasurer or during his own time as prime minister.

The transition to free-market economics in the eastern European bloc and South America was directed by economics professors from Harvard possessed by free-market fervour and armed with a mountain of International Monetary Fund and World Bank cash. Their evangelical spearhead was closely followed by a vanguard of American companies willing to pay cash for what was still state-owned infrastructure.

The Soviet Union in the late 1980s and South America in the early 1990s experienced a massive crisis in banking and business confidence, followed by a stock-market plunge and a freezing of capital movements. This was followed by a bailout with major market-reconstruction strings attached. With the benefit of hindsight, it sounds like an early and more limited version of the global financial disaster, except that America wasn't one of the basket cases.

It must have been an exciting time. A client of mine, who was the finance director for a global oil company, told me about buying infrastructure assets in Russia in the Perestroika days. They would fly into the country with suitcases full of American dollars, using their aircraft fleet of 22 planes and helicopters.

Major state infrastructure assets passed from the Russian government to individuals who very quickly became billionaires, either through the on-sale of the assets or by keeping ownership of key assets.

Britain had its own fiercely committed free marketeer in Margaret Thatcher. She didn't need convincing with a cash handout, and didn't sell state assets to her cronies or keep part of the proceeds. Nor does she own a football club. Her ruthless crushing of the miners' strike by the police in 1984–85 will never be forgotten.

The Keating years in Australia were notable for 21 per cent commercial interest rates, 18 per cent housing-mortgage interest rates, the recession we had to have, the rise and rise of Macquarie Bank, private-public partnerships, compulsory superannuation, and the privatisation and sale of major public assets. This is not a list of positive achievements.

Floating the dollar would generally be regarded by most people as the single unequivocal success of the Keating government. But this wasn't original either. It occurred at a time when a number of currencies were being floated, following immense pressure from the United States, which had become the only superpower in the world.

India, Ghana, Canada, Nigeria, Thailand, Malaysia, Indonesia, and the Philippines all floated their exchange rates in the late 1980s and early 1990s. The Asian currencies were then attacked by the US billionaire speculator George Soros, who almost single-handedly demonstrated that weak, floating currencies were vulnerable to speculative attack. This wasn't much different from our recent experience, when speculators have sold shares that they didn't own (that is, they engaged in what is known as 'shorting' stock), and thereby weakened the viability of substantial companies to a point where their continued existence was threatened.

The currency floats created a new industry, which is now possibly the largest financial-service industry in the world. This is the derivatives business, where you can have a bet on the future rise or fall of any commodity, currency, or event. At the most recent count, the global trade in derivatives each year was worth $US600 trillion, or many times the total income of all the nations in the world. (Some pundits are estimating that it is worth a quadrillion dollars—a thousand trillion dollars.

The introduction of floating exchange rates completely annihilated the economic theory that movements in exchange rates reflected the relative strengths and weaknesses of an economy vis a vis other economies at a given point in time. The derivatives market is, in fact, the biggest gambling den that the world has ever seen.

The Australian dollar, which is traded in pairs against the US dollar and the Japanese yen, is now the fifth-largest currency (by trade value) traded in the world. All the big banks, financial institutions, superannuation funds, the Reserve Bank, and international trading companies are participants. For some players—such as AWA and Pasminco—the currency game overshadowed their real business purpose, and led to their demise or decline.

In the decade of the 1990s and the first seven years of this century, the government, Treasury, and the media believed that the new economy was the way forward. Australia was to be led by the services sector and double-degree bilingual graduates. The old economy of mineral resources, agriculture, and manufacturing — and steady, stable growth — was finished. Any dissidents were marginalised.

The public service was more interested in deregulation than regulation, and Keating's view was that private enterprise could look after its own affairs. The Australian Securities Investment Commission and the Australian Competition and Consumer Commission didn't do much to interfere. When Keating floated the Australian dollar, he said to his principal adviser, Don Russell (recalled in *Confessions of A Bleeding Heart* by Keating's speechwriter, Don Watson), that 'they had done more to de-spiv the Australian economy that day than anyone ever had'. The opposite was actually true. They had created an entirely new and more destructive class of spivs in the financial-services sector.

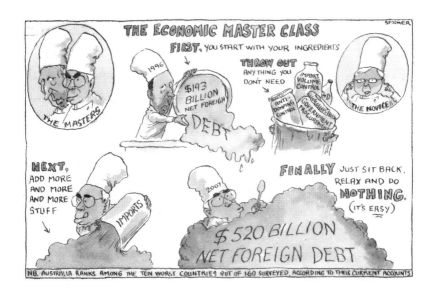

It took a global financial disaster to expose the fact that the rampant stock-market growth of the previous five years after the tech wreck was a deceptive edifice, built on either very little or nothing at all.

The new economy was just another South Sea Bubble led by speculators who repeated the kind of 18th-century London stock-market offering of a company whose prospectus stated that the company's trading intentions would not be disclosed to the shareholders, and which still managed to raise millions of pounds at the height of the frenzy. Few people knew about collateralised debt obligations and derivatives, and even fewer understood what they meant and how they worked.

In this brave old world, financial entrepreneurs such as Babcock & Brown, and Allco, managed to lose close to ten billion dollars in one year.

The new economy spawned a new elite in treasury, academia, and the financial-services sector. That elite had been growing increasingly powerful for the previous 40 years.

The elite is composed of a public-service, academic, consulting, and financial-services technostructure that even John Kenneth Galbraith didn't envisage. The process began as a benign, scientific process of analysis and inquiry that led to proposals for change and improvements in productivity, undertaken by genuine servants of the Australian public. But it has transmuted into a disconnected and powerful elite who ignore popular attitudes as being trivial 'populism', marginalise any dissident thought, and reward those who believe and think 'the right way'. They define the right way as intellectual rigour combined with a fundamentalist belief in the power of the market.

It is worth spending a little space discussing Galbraith's

concept of the 'technostructure', which he detailed in his book *The New Industrial State* (1967). It explains how the academics and the clerks of our society have become so powerful.

Galbraith invented the word 'technostructure' to describe the group of people who are usually the architects of the important decisions made by every large company and government department. They are the people who have spent months or years developing data, analysing it, and presenting recommendations to their senior managements or ministers.

According to Galbraith, members of the technostructure are the real decision-makers. They can leave out data, analysis, and arguments, or distort them to support whatever recommendations they want to make. Generally, politicians, board members, and senior business executives have no ability to challenge the technostructure's arguments and supporting data and analysis that lead to the recommendations. They don't have the time to spend reviewing the issues, or to critically examine the recommendations of the team.

A major policy review may consume years or even decades of research and analysis. How can any individual compete with this, and find the gumption to reject the group recommendations? Ministers, chief executive officers, and boards often don't understand the technical aspects of a project; they have to accept whatever interpretation is given to them by the technostructure.

Most of us generally don't know about or understand the range and complexity of the policies and administrative issues managed by a government department. There is no way that an individual could become competent and knowledgeable about all of the responsibilities of a federal government department, or keep up to date with new responsibilities such as heightened border protection or the technology providing linked databases that might be used in a number of locations, including overseas.

The Australian Customs Service is a good example. It is responsible for the control of all imported and exported goods; it has a major border-security function; it tries to prevent the importation of illicit drugs; and it manages the flow of arrivals and departures at international airports and ports.

These broad functions involve sub-functions: valuing goods; undertaking tariff classifications, using a global system (the Bretton Woods Agreement, which resulted in border-control systems for most countries after 1948); initiating prosecutions; searching baggage, people, and ships; investigating claims of dumping and fraud; collecting revenue; and a host of other sub-activities and sub-sub activities.

Additionally, since the 11 September attack on the World Trade Center, Customs authorities all over the world have been deeply involved in border security. Since that day, the Australian Customs and Border Protection Service (no longer just the Customs Service) has increased its staffing levels by 1500 people. Previously, the reduction of tariff barriers and other trade-liberalisation measures had resulted in a decline in Customs staff levels.

No individual can get across all of these functions, principles, and goals in a lifetime. I have spent a working life trying, and am certainly not an all-round Customs expert.

My first senior work as a public servant involved writing correspondence for Don Chipp, who was minister for customs and excise. He had a specific interest in only two policy issues: drugs and censorship. They had the most electoral impact, and that was all that he and his advisers were interested in.

He had absolutely no understanding of or interest in virtually all the departmental policies and functions for which he was nominally the decision-maker. We made the decisions for him, and he rubber-stamped them.

I have never been to a meeting with ministers where advisers and public servants were not present; often, the minister's only contribution has been to say 'Hello' and 'Goodbye'. I appreciate that captains of industry have private audiences with political decision-makers, but I wonder about the efficacy of such meetings. The billionaire or CEO often isn't across the detail of what he wants to know or ask for, and the minister doesn't necessarily know what he is talking about, and may have difficulty relaying the substance and purpose of the meeting to his advisers.

Some of these meetings involve more ritual than substance. The important point is that the minister or prime minister is prepared to have a face-to-face meeting, and so is the captain of industry. The technocrats from both sides can then determine the outcome with the physical blessing of their respective bosses.

For the past 30 years, the technostructure triumvirate of Treasury, Foreign Affairs and Trade, and the Productivity Commission has created and implemented Australian industry policy. These technocrats have often spent their adult lives in Canberra, and have no major first-hand experience working in any of the substantial industry sectors that contribute to our gross domestic product and the growth of the economy.

In too many cases, young, talented people enter unions and the public service, and go on to become consultants in major economic consultancies, and advisers to parliamentarians, ministers, and shadow ministers. It is almost a closed shop, run and staffed by a disconnected elite.

This phenomenon is present in both state and federal politics. The leaders of student politics invariably join a party in their teens, and are well placed and well connected in their party by their early thirties.

Industry responses to public-service technocrats haven't changed much since my meeting with the senior managers of BHP in 1975. They are not obsequious, but they generally do not bite the hand that they hope will feed them. Few managing directors are prepared to challenge the opinions of the Bright Young Things, in case they are dismissed out of hand as protectionist revisionists seeking rent. The language is almost Stalinist or Maoist.

I have always admired the Japanese process whereby business and the Ministry of International Trade and Industry constantly exchange staff a long way up the career ladder. We tried this in the federal public service during the late 1980s and early 1990s at middle-management levels: the staff seconded to business never came back, while the business people seconded to the public service were ostracised and placed in Coventry; with an eye to the future, they didn't complain, but left as fast as they could.

The seductive quality of the senior public-service departments is that they give young, talented people a taste of real power without them having had the experience necessary to manage it. For many, this power is more important than money. The experience often transmutes into political ambitions.

The second economic-policy power group in Australia is made up of accountants, ex-public servants, and academics. The biggest shift in the consultancy markets has been from private companies to consultants within the first-tier accounting firms; to university consultancies, often chaired by a senior professor; and to consultancies owned by and employing ex-public servants.

This shift is a consequence of the never-ending passion of major accounting firms to expand their income base, the need for universities to generate more income, and the public service's and business's recognition that academic and ex-public servant consultancies will generally end up reaching the conclusions and recommendations that they were pointed to by the government department. It would be instructive to total the many hundreds of millions of dollars in fees paid annually to accountancy firms, ex-public servants, and academic consultancies by state and federal government departments.

These relationships are insidious and difficult to untangle, and they can be unethical. The movement of ex-premiers and ex-ministers to consultancies is often nothing more than a door-opening exercise to the offices of their former colleagues. Part of the power game is to accumulate favours from your colleagues. Such favours have no use-by date.

The financial-services sector, the big end of town, and political players are all part of what has been the greatest boys' (and girls') club of all time. Free-market economics has been their catch cry for avoiding regulation and transparency. The creation of a culture of movement from university politician to adviser to member of parliament to minister to door opener for big business is one of the most obvious forms of corruption in our time.

Chapter Six

The Contribution of Multinationals to Our Foreign Debt

Multinational firms engage in more than 60 per cent of international merchandise trade, and significantly more of the global trade in intangibles and intellectual property. Their business model has shifted irreversibly from locating in high-wage countries that come with costly environmental restrictions and aggressive, mature taxation authorities to locating in countries where labour costs are low, transfer-pricing practices are not closely scrutinised, they are given tax concessions, and they operate with very flexible environmental policies. This may change in the medium term, if they focus on creating employment in their home countries, or the Chinese and Indian economies change their approach to environmental constraints and taxation.

It is a fact that multinationals as a group manage to arrange their affairs in ways that assist them to avoid the company taxation levels borne by companies that have no cross-border affiliates.

The most common way for them to do this is by the head office or its offshore affiliates charging its own entities more for goods and services than they could charge a company at arms' length from them. This results in the Australian entity making less profit and thereby paying less tax. It also results in the inflation of import prices and, in some cases, the deflation of export prices. At an economy-wide level, both events increase the amount of the deficit in the current account and the size of our foreign debt.

The creation of income through a debt obligation allows the multinational to create credit: simply put, multinational and other companies with long trading histories can borrow against their unsold inventories or their balance sheets. Most multinationals have been in business for a long time, and their products have global brand names. As a result, local banks are willing to accept letters of comfort from a multinational to provide funds to an affiliate in virtually every country. The credit can be used to purchase assets in that country.

Australia is a wonderfully stable, attractive country with a long-term history of governments that don't repudiate international debt, nationalise businesses, or appropriate property. We are an ideal investment destination. The only problem is that, as our successful exporting businesses and local suppliers are bought by overseas-owned multinationals, we are exporting less and importing more, including products and brands we used to manufacture—and increasing our debt.

It is likely that the total debt which Australian affiliates owe to their multinational parents is not reflected in annual current-account deficits or the calculation of our foreign debt. In this era of technology-intensive accounting and cross-border communications, we would have no idea of the obligations for, in particular, service payments, intellectual property, and interest that have been accepted by a multinational affiliate but never paid.

The move by the Australian Taxation Office and accounting firms away from the analysis of individual transactions (except in ATO audits and major reviews) has been inevitable. There are simply too many transactions and too many international arrangements between affiliates where the ATO only knows details of half of the deal.

The multinational firm has a further major taxation advantage. The Australian taxation system is based on the self-assessment principle, and audits of the taxpayer affiliates are arduous and uncommon: the average transfer-pricing audit takes two-and-a-half years. In the meantime, company-initiated annual returns are merely summaries of total income and expenditure. They do not provide transactional information, yet the devil may be in that hidden detail.

An affiliate that has lost money for a long time may simply be closed by the parent company, along with its accumulated losses. It is extremely unlikely that an audit of a defunct company would be undertaken in the parent company's home jurisdiction to explain why the parent company had closed a defunct loss-making company. Alternatively, the company might change from operating as a manufacturer to becoming an importer. The accumulated losses could then be offset against profits from importing derived in future years.

***

Transfer pricing by multinational companies is a simple strategic concept that has been employed for at least a century.

Prices charged between affiliates are, by definition, not set at arms' length. If the parent company wants to, it can structure prices for cross-border transfers between its wholly owned affiliates in different countries so that one makes a lot of profit and the other makes a loss. Over time, the loss would be intolerable for the buyer if the companies were buying and selling at arms' length. However, the loser may borrow for years if it is supported by the parent company to obtain credit.

This ability to manipulate prices is then combined with the opportunities to pay less tax in various places, to never bring the income home, or to take advantage of tax holidays or incentives provided by various countries.

There are 10,000 subsidiaries of multinationals operating in Australia. More than 95 per cent of them are marketers and distributors that import and sell the goods and services created by other affiliates in other countries. Their parent companies are usually European, American, Japanese, and Korean entities. Incredibly, there are no contemporary statistics regarding their share of Australia's national income.

Transfer pricing is not illegal, but the tax authorities of the world want resident companies to pay a fair share of tax to their national treasuries. Tax authorities attempt to achieve this goal by using a well-developed method: they examine the cross-border sales and purchases of products and services between affiliates, and relate them to an external pricing standard that is called 'the arms' length principle'. This principle is based on the idea that companies dealing with each other across national borders that have no ownership connection will charge and pay a price that delivers a fair profit to each of them and covers all their costs, having regard to domestic market conditions.

Before 1990, most multinationals created different prices for different national markets that had regard to the level of domestic competition and tariff barriers. The intention was still to structure the affiliates' profit in such a way that little or no tax was paid.

Most multinational affiliates are marketer-distributors. A major multinational might have 150 subsidiary affiliates around the world, but only four or five of them might be manufacturing affiliates; the balance of affiliates simply import, market, and distribute the global products.

Manufacturing is normally located in the parent company's home country and in countries (such as Ireland, Singapore, Malaysia, and Puerto Rico) that provide specific taxation incentives for manufacturing and for the liberal treatment of income from intangibles.

Parent functions include intangibles such as research and development, manufacturing know-how, IT systems, marketing strategies, and distribution systems. They may also lend or guarantee loans to their affiliates if the latter are losing money. Affiliate functions include manufacturing, marketing, logistics, warehousing, accounting and credit control, and management.

Australian multinational subsidiaries often provide much of the management and technical-compliance functions for New Zealand, which is generally treated as a seventh state of Australia for multinational affiliates' management purposes.

The parent assets sold, leased, or charged to affiliates include the ownership of logos, patents, copyrights, properties, marketing, and logistics systems, and any other plant, equipment, or other tangible capital equipment.

The risks shared between the parent and the affiliates

include movements in the exchange rate, bad debts, product failures, warranty claims, product recalls, and any other risk that companies normally have to bear in business.

All of these activities can be affected by transfer-pricing practices. To investigate them, the categories of income generation and expenditure are combined in what is called a functional analysis — a task that is performed by the tax authorities, and may also be undertaken by the multinationals and their affiliates. Most major multinationals have documentation prepared to support their transfer-pricing policies. Interestingly, there are very few assumptions used in this process. It is, rather, about the facts and the numbers involved in a transaction between affiliated parties.

Functional analysis is employed to calculate what should be the arms' length price of the company's range of products or services. The calculation of this price involves a number of methodologies that have been developed and agreed to by most industrial nations over the past 40 years to help standardise the analytical approach of the national tax authorities and the conclusions they draw from it.

The Organisation for Economic and Cultural Development (OECD) was the major international co-ordinator of this project. The ATO, the US Internal Revenue Service (IRS), the European tax authorities, and the National Tax Office of Japan were heavily involved in the substantial conceptual development of the principles and methodologies of transfer pricing. This process of development and agreement between the members of the OECD continues to the present.

The need for in-depth industry analysis and the creation of substantial submissions on an industry or particular company suited my work skills and background — I had been learning about this from the time I first made submissions for Customs to the Public Service Board explaining what Customs did and why they should (always) get more staff of a higher level.

In 1989, our Deloitte's business unit's transfer-pricing experience began with a major case involving Yamaha and the IRS. Ernie Sharkey and I had won Yamaha as a client, and had worked for them on dumping and other major Customs matters in our own consultancy for a number of years.

Yamaha became embroiled in a major dispute with the IRS about company tax and the losses that the company had experienced over the previous 15 years. The IRS had assessed Yamaha for $650 million in taxes, interest, and penalties.

The US attitude was that Yamaha Japan had been forcing Yamaha USA to hold massive stocks of motorcycles that couldn't be sold for years. According to the IRS, the cost of holding the inventory in America deliberately destroyed the profitability of Yamaha's US subsidiary.

The real reason for the losses, though, was that motorcycle riders all over the world had worked out that motorcycles were dangerous (the death rate per thousand was more than twice the highest death rate for particular models of passenger motor vehicles). This resulted in a massive drop globally in consumer demand in the late 1970s and 1980s for motorcycles, and a consequent major increase in unsold stock. Yamaha, Honda, and Kawasaki all experienced the same reduction in demand, and panicked. The consequence was what came to be called the motorcycle wars. Yamaha's inventory problems arose from the intense competition that occurred in the market.

The IRS and Yamaha eventually reached a settlement, for a fraction of the amount originally sought by the IRS. Our submission, using the Australian motorcycle market as a comparison to the US market, was very valuable. We argued that there were profitable independent state distributors in Australia who were paying import prices to Yamaha that were higher than the prices paid by the US subsidiary. On this evidence, it was difficult for the IRS to claim that Yamaha, the parent company, was overcharging its subsidiaries to keep the profit in Japan.

The ATO commenced a review of 750 multinational affiliates in Australia in 1990. From that review emerged an audit programme of major multinational companies that is still continuing. It is no wonder that Michael Carmody, who was the taxation commissioner at the time, said that transfer pricing was the tax issue of the 1990s.

During that period, I was the national director of transfer pricing in both Deloitte and Ernst & Young. Transfer pricing developed into a major client service provided by the first-tier accounting firms. They had almost a total lock on the market, as they generally provided audit and other accounting services on a global basis to virtually all of the multinationals included in the ATO's audit program.

Within the major accounting firms, the emphasis was on creating documents that demonstrated how the affiliate and its offshore parent or associate had arrived at prices that were based on the arms' length principle. Usually this involved a functional analysis to explain to the ATO the nature of the business activity in Australia and how the Australian entity was compensated for the functions it performed, the assets it contributed, and the risks that it took.

Our idea was to make sure that the ATO didn't chase red herrings, and that it was properly informed as to the businesses' activities.

In the early days, the ATO interviewed non-English-speaking executives, and this was often a case of those who couldn't explain talking to those who didn't understand. The result was one-page interview reports by the ATO that covered interviews which may have lasted two hours. Some of the ATO international tax audits took over ten years to complete. This obviously created massive contingent liabilities for the taxpayer, and substantial issues of fairness and equity for the ATO.

In the late 1990s, the ATO commissioned me to write a manual for transfer pricing by marketer-distributors. At the same time, I began working as the only Australian independent expert for the ATO in major reviews and audit disputes. I was also a member of the transfer pricing sub-committee of the ATO's taxation committee, which was responsible for the development and publication of a series of public rulings on transfer-pricing issues that constituted more than half of the public rulings issued by the ATO in the 1990s.

The ATO and the major accounting firms heartily endorsed my working for both sides, as it helped each of them understand the other. A lot of time and money was spent in the early days of transfer-pricing reviews simply because there was often a siege mentality in the company and its advisers, and misunderstandings about what the relationships between affiliates were really about.

My philosophy was the same as it had been in my submissions of evidence to the Industries Commission: it was about telling the truth, and doing the best you could for the client in the context of the law and the rulings. The sooner the job was finished, the sooner the affiliate could go about its normal business, and the sooner the ATO could move onto the next case. At no stage did I want anyone (on either side) to be able to say that my work had dudded them.

From 1990 until the early 2000s, the topic resulted in the publication of thousands of pages of public rulings dealing with the entire range of transfer-pricing issues and the processes that should be adopted by companies to ensure that they could demonstrate that they were low risk for the purposes of the ATO.

This was a good and transparent process because it meant that the ATO clearly and publicly identified and discussed its approach, principles, and suggested review-structures with target companies. The ATO then conducted a major series of seminars and workshops that must have cost it some millions of dollars.

As a result, there is really no longer any justification for any multinational affiliate company pleading ignorance about transfer pricing and the forms of contemporaneous documentation and transaction records that the ATO requires from prudent businessmen aware of their tax obligations.

Australian affiliates should have at their disposal, at a bare minimum, a brief explanation of the functions they perform, the financial risks they bear, and the assets they contribute. They should also be able to explain what their overseas affiliate does and contributes towards the transaction. They should know the basic elements of the methodologies used to compare their pricing against the arms' length standard, and they should be able to show the ATO their policy documents which demonstrate that they have been acting in accordance with that standard to arrive at prices paid or received from their overseas affiliates.

Much of the work that led to this understanding inevitably involved the overseas parent company, which wanted to keep a very careful eye on the outcome of any review by the ATO. Australia was a leading light in the OECD negotiations from 1970 to 1990, and is still an influential participant in the OECD working parties. Its perspective would influence tax-authority deliberations in a number of countries.

This period was also the start of a direct exchange of information between the ATO, the IRS, and the tax authorities in New Zealand, the UK, and Japan. This sort of transparency meant that the tax auditors were able to see both ends of a transaction.

This international initiative exposes as fallacious the concern that some people have expressed about transfer-pricing actions by the ATO. They do not frighten multinationals into moving offshore, as there is no country of substance for them to operate in that doesn't employ the OECD transfer-pricing principles.

Transfer pricing is probably the biggest single source of our foreign debt. Many multinational affiliates have been paying more than the arms' length price for imports from their overseas affiliates, and are consequently in break-even or loss situations when they should be profitable. They remain viable only through the financial support of their parent companies. This statement is not an assertion — details are available regarding the aggregate value of settlements resulting from transfer-pricing audits by the ATO over the past 15 years. Additionally, the audited companies have changed their transactional relationships with their parent companies and affiliates.

Getting additional tax paid is a good result for the ATO's transfer-pricing program, but even better is the resulting annual increase in income in Australia and the decrease in payments made to overseas affiliates. This impacts directly on our current-account deficit.

***

The Australian Bureau of Statistics (ABS) yearbook for 2008 is the most recent aggregate source of information for Australia's nett foreign debt, which is the difference between our lending to overseas entities and residents and our borrowing from them. This number should not be confused with the debt arising from our excess of imported goods and services over exports.

The foreign-direct-investment statistics are, according to the ABS, 'a category of international investment that reflects the objective of obtaining a lasting interest by a resident of one economy in an enterprise in another economy' (*Yearbook Australia 2008*).

In the five years to 2007, our foreign-debt liabilities increased from $583 billion to $972 billion, and our assets rose in value from $226 billion to $428 billion. The nett foreign debt of the private sector was $559 billion, while the public sector actually had a small surplus.

Much of the gross investment in the three years to 2007 would have come from the United States.

On 1 January 2005, the USAFTA (United States–Australia Free Trade Agreement) came into operation. The Institute of Public Affairs (a major, global free-market think tank) claims that the real purpose of the USAFTA was to free up investment in Australia by the US and, presumably, vice versa. If this was true, I don't know why both sides bothered spending so much time discussing and negotiating merchandise-trade issues, intellectual property, the Pharmaceutical Benefits Scheme, and local content in the performing arts.

The US has been investing freely in Australia ever since Britain joined the Common Market in the 1960s. The bigger our trade deficit with the US gets, the more they have used the surplus to buy up Australian land and companies.

I am also very suspicious of the authenticity of the numbers used to compare the two-way flow of investment funds between Australia and the United States. Just before and since the introduction of the USAFTA, the relevant numbers (expressed in US billions of dollars) were as follows:

	Australian investment in the US	US investment in Australia
2002	214	245
2003	239	296
2004	287	370
2005	309	340
2006	338	379
2007	414	435

On the numbers, the growth trend in investment isn't significant either way. It certainly doesn't match the percentage growth in merchandise trade and the nett services-and-income deficit.

My reservation is that our companies investing in the US are either Australian in name only or have a very substantial number of foreign investors in their share registry. Most US investors in Australia don't have Australian shareholders. Companies such as News Limited are hardly Australian. Thirty per cent of BHP Billiton's shares are held by foreign investors.

The ABS has published some interesting statistics about

foreign investment in Australia. In 2002, overseas residents held 29 per cent of the equity on issue in Australian enterprise groups; local residents held the balance of 71 per cent. The total value of equity on issue was $1.2 trillion. In 2007, the foreign/domestic split was precisely the same, but the equity on issue had grown to $2.2 trillion.

Of course, there are no equity-issue values for the subsidiaries of foreign multinationals, as they are almost always 100 per cent owned by their overseas parents. However, Australian minority shareholders have occasionally caused problems for them.

For example, after the Bhopal tragedy, Union Carbide sold many of its affiliates, including Eveready batteries — but wasn't aware that some of the shares in the company were still owned by Australian and New Zealand interests. The latter group successfully negotiated to obtain the Australian GLAD business as compensation for the Eveready shares that Union Carbide had sold when it hadn't owned them.

On this basis, it is not hard to conclude that overseas residents own more than half of the equity in companies operating in Australia. I don't see why the Institute of Public Affairs thinks that we have to free up foreign investment any more than we already have in Australia.

We do need to get a clear and simple understanding of what the level of foreign ownership of companies is in Australia. There is a great competitive advantage to a multinational in being able to source with certainty from your affiliates, to have no credit risk, and to be able to obtain financing on a global basis. When taxation benefits are added to this mix, it becomes an irresistible proposition.

Australia should take a leaf out of President Obama's book. The prime minister should publicly state what profits are being made by Australia's largest 100 companies, who they are, and how much tax they are paying. These companies have been part of a major review by the ATO during the past 20 years. It would also be interesting to know what additional tax they paid as a consequence of the review.

***

The Australian economy stands at a watershed: the steps we take today will determine its direction over the next 50 years. We have little government foreign debt (between $300 and $400 billion—most countries have foreign debts equal to or greater than a year's national income), and we are constantly being reminded by the politicians that we have missed a bullet from the global financial disaster. But that was really the preliminary tsunami. The major economic tsunami that is roaring down upon us is a combination of our systemic current-account deficit and the $700 billion we owe to overseas lenders. We have eliminated or reduced most of our avenues of escape from this tidal wave.

Our ten mortal policy-sins have been:

1. The 30-year decline in Australian manufacturing;
2. The sale of the most successful Australian brand names and exporters to multinationals;
3. The elimination of trade barriers and the absence of any significant non-tariff measures to replace them;
4. A taxation differential between local companies and foreign companies;
5. Government resistance to the promotion of Australian-made products;
6. The elimination of any government preference to Australian companies;
7. The failure of the government to mount a comprehensive review of transfer-pricing practices. For 20 years, it has been left to whatever initiatives a single government agency, the ATO, has been willing and able to mount;
8. Increasing interest payments on a growing foreign debt;
9. Increasing numbers of multinational subsidiaries locating in Australia and replacing arms' length marketer-distributors; and
10. The sale of major infrastructure to pay off the debts of the state and federal governments.

Some of these policies have been forced upon us. Some of

them have been entered into with our eyes wide open. Some have been welcomed.

The influx of capital investment has certainly internationalised the Australian economy. The questions that have never been answered, however, are, 'When is enough enough?' and 'How fast should we grow?' Uncontrollable growth is epitomised by the trade in derivatives and the US housing bubble. At some stage, we will have nothing left to sell, and will be unable to earn sufficient income in the domestic market to pay for the imports we want to buy.

There will always be some — the inheritors, the clever, the young and educated, and the lucky — who can't see or understand the problem. There won't be a recession for them, and the more obtuse amongst them will wonder if the recession really exists at all and whether the losers have 'deserved to lose'. This is an elitist perspective that very few Australians had 30 years ago.

The global financial disaster may be the catalyst for change. There is no doubt — and the banks acknowledge this — that we have accumulated an amount of foreign debt which is payable to foreign lenders that they may not all be willing or able to roll over.

We are also accumulating new public foreign debt through federal government initiatives designed to assist our people and our companies survive the worst of the global recession. That debt presently stands at approximately $300 billion. Other countries may be worse off, but their current-account deficit is a lot lower than ours.

The solution to this is simple, but seems to be unachievable. We have to consume fewer imports of goods and services, and export more. There is no other way.

Ultimately, our present policy is a road to national impoverishment and the transformation of Australia into a third-world economy. The larger our foreign debt, the less likely we are to obtain globally the further credit we need; and the less credit available to us, the less economic activity there will be, and the less tax revenue there will be to fund government services. We will only have new resource-discoveries and agricultural produce left to sell. This may not be the immediate prospect facing the Baby Boomers, but it is not many generations away. The global financial disaster has accelerated the approach of this scenario.

Chapter Seven
The Global Financial Disaster of 2007–09

In the First and Second World Wars, nearly every Australian family had a husband, brother, son, or cousin at Gallipoli, in France, in the European battlefields, in the African desert, in the jungles of New Guinea, or on the Pacific islands. The deep hurt caused by the deaths of some of these soldiers, and the serious injuries and emotional damage suffered by others, reached out and touched every family — and keeps doing so, to the present day. We all know what happened (some better than others) and what the wars cost.

The impact of the global financial disaster is probably even more widespread. Yet many Australians don't know what has happened and how it has directly impacted on them or those they care about. Some people have lost money in the share market, so at least they know about that. But we have all lost part of our compulsory superannuation payments made over the past ten years. Many part-time employees have been dismissed without any entitlements, and many full-time employees will be next.

Housing prices are up, but we are creating our own mini-housing bubble. Minus the fraud and the NINJA loans, this is still a major problem for the future. As a consequence of low interest rates and the temporary government stimulus (which was equivalent to a deposit on low-cost homes), Australians who could never afford to buy have bought into the market or upgraded on the basis that low interest rates meant they could afford a more expensive home. Those rates have already gone, and all borrowers are now having to deal with rising rates.

Finally, reduced government taxation revenue will result from a smaller national income and lower company profits or losses. Concomitantly, the social-security budget will have to increase to meet the needs of those newly out of work.

The government has also reintroduced government debt. This time, unlike during the 1990 recession, we do not have major assets such as Telstra, electricity and water authorities, and roads and railways to sell. They have already been sold to pay off the debt that all Australian governments incurred during the good times.

The present nett federal government debt is $300 billion. There are no numbers available for state government debt as they try to grapple with increased social services and decreased state taxation revenue.

The size of superannuation losses is making some people realise that they will have to work at least another two years to try to restore their funds. The loss may be as much as one-third of our savings, but many people don't want to know how much—and the superannuation funds aren't volunteering the information. Many retirees are reducing their standards of living to match the reduced level of their superannuation income.

The government will also legislate to increase both the minimum-age requirement for the old-age pension and for superannuation entitlements. The ageing of the Australian population, the reduction in the birth rate, and the massive increase in Pharmaceutical Benefits System costs is creating a pressure on government funds that is destroying the old paradigms for social-welfare payments in Australia.

One other major difference between this recession and the recessions of the 1970s and 1990s is its universality: it is affecting nearly every economy and everybody in the world.

The behaviour demonstrated by some major players in the US's financial-services sector who created the global financial disaster has been on show before in Australia. It is amazing how people forget (or never know about) financial scams that once had the appearance of integrity because they involved some of the four major banks. Over 20 years ago, for example, some of the major banks offered farmers and property-owners loans in Swiss francs secured against their properties. The Australian interest rate was about 9 per cent at the time, and the interest rate for Swiss francs that the banks could borrow at was about 2–3 per cent. The banks offered these loans to its local customers at around 6–7 per cent. For the banks, the 4–5 per cent difference between the costs of funds and the price of the loan was money for jam. For the borrower, this was much cheaper money than was available from local sources.

This sounded great. The only problem was that few of the participants worried about the possibility or consequences of adverse movements in the exchange rate between the Swiss franc and the Australian dollar. Most farmers had no idea of the risks they had exposed themselves to, and most bankers didn't bother to warn them. The rate at the time was 2.5 Swiss francs to the dollar. So when a farmer borrowed a million Australian dollars, he or she had in fact borrowed 2.5 million Swiss francs to get access to the funds — and the loan eventually would have to be repaid in the latter currency, whatever the ruling exchange rate was.

Within a few years the Swiss franc indeed began moving adversely — eventually, to less than parity with the dollar. This meant that some farmers had to pay back more than $A2.5 million plus interest to meet their obligations on a loan of $1 million. Alternatively, the bank would sell the farm.

This particular piece of deception, which traded on the ignorance of farmers and exploited the ethical reputation of banks, only differs from the current era's low-doc loans and collateralised debt securities by the size of the scam and the circumstances of the borrowers. Some of the victims had money, and took the matter to court: some of the court cases were settled, some were won, some were lost, and some are probably still in litigation. It all depended on individual representations and contractual detail, and the depth of the plaintiff's pockets.

There was much grief caused, and probably a couple of hundred million dollars lost, as a result of the Swiss loans' debacle, which at least some of the farmers had the will and the resources to fight. To this day, no one in the general public knows who lost their property as a consequence of the affair.

If we fast-forward to the current disaster, the financial sector in the US wrote $US1.3 trillion in sub-prime mortgage loans that are basically now worth nothing. This is 8000 times the amount written in the Australian–Swiss loans' debacle (having regard to the $A–$US exchange-rate difference). The US financial sector managed to spread its risk around the world. Everybody bought some of the clever, pretty paper; their financial investment models told them that they had to.

As time passes, it will be instructive to see how much litigation through class actions emerges out of the global financial disaster. There is nothing in it for the class-action litigators representing the mortgagees who have nothing: no job, and no equity in their houses. As the entirety of the losses and financial obligations becomes known, we will see other groups of borrowers and investors who either did have some house equity or did buy toxic collateralised debt obligations (CDOs) with their AAA ratings. Class actions are now commonplace in the US and are becoming common in Australia.

While the general public has a tendency to forget about financial disasters after several years have elapsed, the lawyers who run class actions on a contingency basis don't have the same attitude at all.

The first Australian class action of the sub-prime era that has been widely publicised has been launched by the local councils that invested $700 million with Lehman Brothers, and who have been fobbed off with an offer of between 3 and 13 cents while the American creditors get 42 cents in the dollar. The reason for this is the claim that the councils are only 'contingent' creditors (that is, payments are only to be made to them after the first tier of American creditors has been satisfied). That's a great half-billion dollar word.

Understanding and explaining the causes of the financial meltdown, first in the United States and then in the rest of the industrial economies, is like trying to deal with the causes of World War I. There were specific events, central ideologies, and major players involved.

The financial bonfire began in the US in what is called the sub-prime loans market — which is a euphemism for high-risk loans enabled by a mountain of very low-interest money available from the US central bank and Japan. The interest rate was 1 per cent or even lower for Japanese yen.

A July 2009 Federal Reserve Bank of New York staff report (no. 382), by Adrian Tobias and Hyun Song Shin, provides a good explanation of what they call the 'shadow banking system' and its implications for financial regulation. The authors make the point that, while banks in the US have been the dominant suppliers of credit throughout the country, they have been increasingly supplanted by market-based institutions, especially those involved in the securitisation process. (Securitisation is the process of parcelling loans — in this case, loans for house purchases — into a package that is then onsold to investors.) The 'securities' are intended to reduce the credit-issuer's risk by being passed on to the next person. In reality, this is very much a massively expensive game of 'Pass the Parcel'.

The packagers were Lehman Brothers, Merrill Lynch, Goldman Sachs, UBS, Credit Suisse, and other smaller Wall Street bankers. The customers for the packagers were pension (that is, superannuation) funds, mutual funds, insurance companies, overseas banks, councils, and foreign central banks, and anybody else with money virtually anywhere in the world. Tobias and Shin state that market-based institutions (that is, not commercial banks) constituted two-thirds of the $11 trillion total of home mortgages in the United States. The Wall Street bankers also increased their potential gains (and losses) by buying securitised packages from each other with borrowed money.

The temptation was irresistible for the fast-money men. Housing prices were increasing in the US; there was a huge, unsatisfied demand for housing from people with poor credit and employment histories; and the lender could foreclose and sell the house if the borrower defaulted. These were called NINJA (no income, no job, no assets) loans. The theory was that, in the event of a loan default, the lenders would get more from the proceeds of the foreclosure sale than from failing to recover the amount of the debt. This opportunity was a licence to print money through high fees and interest rates, and that is exactly what the operators in the US mortgage market did.

The devices used to maximise the money men's revenue included increasing the fees on a loan, resetting the interest rates after a couple of years of payment, and inflating the borrower's income a number of times. This allowed him or her to borrow more (which the borrower neither intended nor had the capacity to repay) and pay higher fees out of the loan amount. One enterprising entrepreneur even organised mortgages for jail inmates: the inmates of one Rocky Mountain penitentiary bought 17 houses with low-doc mortgages.

Believe it or not, some buyers were happy to participate in a 'price puff', whereby the price of the house they were buying was inflated by $100,000, and they received $30,000 of the artificially inflated sale price. Why aren't these people and the people who orchestrated the rort going to jail? If the borrowers had no money, no jobs, and no assets, the $30,000 share of the fraud proceeds must have been manna from heaven to them. Having a house of one's own for a few years, despite the fact that the payments couldn't possibly be met, would be an impoverished person's dream.

The mortgage rates were as high as 7.5 per cent, and would often be reset to 9.5 per cent after two years. This was an unconscionable increase from the original interest cost of 1 per cent or even less that had been paid by the originators of the low-doc schemes.

The final and so far unpunished enticement in the securitised-packages scam was that the cute little bundles were classified as having an AAA rating (that is, the least-risky ranking) by the ratings agencies, Moodys, and Standard & Poor's. These faulty ratings have severely diminished the credibility of the agencies.

Economists and commentators call this on-selling an example of financial players falling prey to 'moral hazard'—succumbing to the temptation to engage in unwise and unethical behaviour, and to take greater risks than is warranted, because they know they won't be held responsible for the consequences of their own actions. The term is used especially in the case of banks thinking that, whatever they do, they'll be bailed out by the government because they're too important and too big to be allowed to fail. In practice, it means that the packagers keep the profits, but the purchasers bear risks that they aren't aware of—and incur the eventual losses. This is a common outcome of public-private partnerships when a particular piece of transport infrastructure doesn't earn the toll or other revenues that were originally modelled by developers and investment banks to justify their acquisition of the publicly held infrastructure. In such circumstances, the state often ends up owning the road or railway or other asset that it thought it was privatising—or has to pay higher subsidies to the private operators, which often negate the privatisation proceeds.

While the toxic assets were being repackaged, internationalised, and offloaded, the housing sales-bubble caused by low-doc loans was forcing interest rates in the US higher. This made it even more unlikely that new recipients of low-doc loans would be able to meet their commitments. The foreclosures started, and the final act of the tragedy for the poor, the foolish, and the desperate was under way. Virtually all such property-owners didn't have the equity to meet their outstanding and rapidly expanding debts.

Many of these houses now stand empty. Many of them were built in isolated, marginal areas, and they have often been vandalised or had their fittings and piping stolen, so resale is generally not an option. The consequence of all this is that the number of foreclosures in the US could increase from one million to eight million houses in the next few years. This means that up to 20 million displaced, poor, and now often-bankrupt Americans will be looking for somewhere to live.

There is no mathematical model in existence that can measure the social cost of this pogrom on the poor in the United States. How many people will commit murder, suicide, or crimes and other acts of violence against their families? How many will end up in jails or institutions as a consequence of the greed of the free-market economists, and their success in getting so many people to 'act rationally in their self-interest'?

No one will measure this cost because they can't make money from the measurement.

Those buying the toxic CDO packages used off-the-shelf mathematical models to value the products. The problem was that the models hadn't assumed the devastating impact on housing prices of a lot of mortgages being foreclosed at the same time. They also hadn't assumed that interest rates would rise and that house prices would fall.

Essentially, greed, deception, and a reckless reliance on economic models that did not relate to the trading environment were the economic iceberg that sank the free-market, sub-prime Titanic.

These events are behind the linked phenomena of your superannuation going down significantly in value, your house prices being propped up by low interest rates that won't last, your share portfolio being in tatters, you having to work longer, and some of you losing your jobs or your overtime. We didn't create the toxic-loan virus, but we created the opportunity for it to be transmitted to Australia.

Many Australians are asking themselves, *What have America's problems got to do with us?* At one level, they're right. Our banks don't fund sub-prime loans, and the Australian mortgage providers that offered the euphemistically titled low-doc loans never acquired more than 10 per cent of the housing-borrower market. The loans they were flogging weren't NINJA mortgages anyway. (Those same non-bank lenders would have a minuscule 5 per cent share now — the crisis-led government guarantee for bank loans has enabled the banks to increase their market share substantially.)

The first strain of the toxic-loan virus to reach Australia was a consequence of our banks' inability to obtain sufficient savings from the local savings pool to provide business and personal credit. Our credit-card debt of over $60 billion is only one example of such debt. Most businesses have working overdrafts that total billions of dollars. And housing-debt mortgages total many tens of billions of dollars.

Australian banks pay little interest on deposits, so they seldom attract domestic savings. The Bendigo Bank is one of the few banks started on the basis of a substantial funding of loans (60 per cent) from a savings model.

This accumulation of business and personal debt in Australia, most of which has not been funded from deposits, has manifested itself as a foreign debt of nearly $700 billion. We have borrowed this money from our own banks, which in turn have had to borrow overseas to be able to meet our demand for credit.

Overseas lenders may not be willing or able to continue to lend us the money to finance our historic and ever-increasing foreign debt. We are at the mercy of their financial circumstances and judgements regarding the value of the securities for our loans.

On 18 June 2009, the *Australian Financial Review* (*AFR*) published a front-page story, followed by a page of commentary, about Australia's current-account deficit (CAD). It was gratifying to see that the *AFR* had finally discovered that both the current-account deficit and the foreign debt are real problems.

Australia's only financial newspaper has been a current-account-deficit sceptic for the past 30 years, and has ignored the foreign debt. The Society for Balanced Trade, founded by Ernest Rodeck and Bill Weekes, had focused on the same issue 20 years before, and as a result had been laughed at and treated as part of the lunatic economic fringe. On 6 August 2009, the *AFR* began a major three-part series on the CAD and also covered the transfer-pricing issue, noting that the ATO had audited 69 companies in the two years from 2007–08 to 2008–09.

It was balm for the Society for Balanced Trade's soul when, in 2008, the prime minister recognised the CAD as one of

Australia's major economic problems. Then, in June 2009, the *AFR* quoted Don Argus, the chairman of Australia's highest-valued company, BHP Billiton, and previously the CEO of the National Australia Bank, as saying that 'the global financial crisis has highlighted one of the long-standing issues of Australia's financial system. This is Australia's reliance on foreign capital ...'

The *AFR* said: 'At its heart is the persistent current account deficit—a two-decade-old phenomenon given a new twist by the credit crunch. Since the 1980s, local investment needs have consistently outstripped savings. As a result, the economy relies on importing savings from offshore to fund its growth.'

The *AFR* went on to quote loan-to-deposit ratios that are probably the worst of all developed countries'. It quoted the International Monetary Fund's warning in 2006 that our banks' reliance on wholesale funding 'makes them more vulnerable to an event such as a ratings downgrade and collectively more vulnerable to an event such as a collapse in commodity pricing that might affect investor sentiment towards Australia'.

As we will see later, the foreign debt arises from a simple fact that, for every quarter since 1973, we have imported more goods and services than we have exported (which thereby creates the current-account deficit).

Consumer products, pharmaceuticals, information technology, motor vehicles, and capital equipment contribute the bulk of the value of our physical imports. Our major exports are metallic ores, minerals, gold, agricultural produce, and some manufactured goods.

The services we import include fees paid by businesses to their overseas parents, technical-service fees, and royalties.

Major exported services are tourism, construction, and education. The education services we 'export' are mostly sold to expatriate students living in Australia.

Even when we had a trade surplus in the short-lived resources export boom, we still ended up in deficit for 2007–08. This was a consequence of the services nett debt and the fact that we are presently paying $50 billion in interest on the foreign debt that we have accumulated over 30 years. So the second strain of the virus emerged from our chronic and endless inability to export more goods and services than we import.

The third strain attacked many of our investment funds, superannuation funds, councils, companies, governments, and who knows what else. These bodies were actively and directly solicited to purchase CDO packages from Credit Suisse, Lehman Brothers, Merrill Lynch, and UBS, etc. Many bought them because they were offered above-market rates of return, and their modelling programmes told them they were good investments providing a greater return than was available elsewhere. In other words, they were promised a greater-than-reasonable return, and they were greedy. It will take a while for the truth to come out about who got caught and for how much.

The fourth strain of the virus resulted in a banking freeze that quickly became a global crisis impacting on any country which had institutions or governments that borrowed internationally. Many of the loans were made with commercial paper that turned over every 90 or 180 days. Participants in the market are banks and other financial institutions that operate with a considerable amount of informality and trust. Normally, they trust the underlying security for the loans, but that trust evaporated in the sub-prime crisis.

The fifth strain of the virus is Australia's banks' and financial institutions' excessive involvement in the global-derivatives markets, particularly the futures trade in the Aussie dollar against the US dollar and the Japanese yen. Our currency is traded in the market in volumes that are frightening, and which are completely divorced from our need to buy or sell foreign exchange to pay for imports or to repatriate foreign currency obtained from export sales.

As we have seen, it has been suggested that the total value of the global-derivatives trade has reached a quadrillion dollars—about the GDP of 800 United States of Americas. I think this would be the first time that this previously theoretical number has had a commercial application. It is equal to the fortunes of a million billionaires.

In 2002, I tried to interest a very senior executive at Westpac in the idea of bundling together currency requirements for a number of large importers, in order to give them a better exchange rate. At the time, Australia needed a total of about $150 billion annually in foreign currency to cover its imports. The country's total imports/exports trade was worth more than this, but some transactions were made in Australian dollars.

The banker told me that this amount was too trifling for them to be bothered with. It was equivalent to about 20 hours of trading by major Australian banks in the derivatives market for the Australian dollar, and represented less than one-third of 1 per cent of the trade in a year. This meant that, even back then, the derivatives trade conducted by the four major banks must have been worth $4.5 trillion—or an amount equivalent to between four and five years of our annual gross national income. I wonder what the trade is worth now; it has grown very quickly since then.

A lot of the derivatives trading is really just about placing a bet. Pasminco was the world's richest lead mine, but it went into administration because its finance team decided they could make more money by betting on exchange-rate movements than by selling lead. AWA was mortally wounded by losses resulting from internal foreign-currency trading.

It's little wonder that US investor Warren Buffett told his Hathaway shareholders that 'derivatives are weapons of mass destruction'. You can bet on just about anything in the future that you care to nominate. Some of the bets are sensible insurance, but my banker's comment shows that most are simply gambling, relying on the usual panoply of mathematical models.

Many organisations and companies have lost a lot of money simply by hedging huge amounts of foreign exchange, for reasons that bear no relation to their usual business activities. The fact is that they have lost sight of their original commercial purposes. Major banks should be interested in deposits, and should pay interest at levels that is sufficient to attract them. They could make more money on occasions by borrowing overseas, but that involves a small detail called 'risk'. That is why the return for doing so is greater. And that is why they have lost large sums of money now. One source at *The Age* has told me that the amount of the sour loans held by the banks ($16.5 billion) is about equal to the combined profits of about $18 billion that they will make over the next several years.

The crisis was a direct consequence of the entrenched theory that the market can do what it likes, whenever it likes, because rational people will always make sensible decisions with perfect knowledge about whether and what to buy or invest. The disciples of this concept rejected any regulation by government to protect the interests of its citizens or to require global companies, their affiliates, and powerful individuals to act other than in their own interest. This was free-market economics in action.

Language is used as a media-spin weapon in economics and in business: multinationals are now 'global companies'; subsidiaries of multinationals are now 'affiliates'; and rational consumers are now 'educated consumers'.

In brutal terms, sub-prime loan marketers were allowed to prey upon people who were too poor to be able to borrow the money to buy a house, and sufficiently naive to not understand how they were being manipulated. There were no Bureaus of Consumer Affairs or Offices of Fair Trading to help them.

In 2007, superannuation funds provided 54 per cent of the venture capital of $7 billion that was identified by the Australian Bureau of Statistics as having been lent to first-tier developers who do not have a market-ready concept or product. I wonder how those investments are performing.

It would also be interesting to know how much of the 27 per cent of the federal government's Future Fund investment in the US was placed in derivatives or collateralised debt obligations. All Australian citizens are entitled to have this information.

The core problems in the crisis were ignorance, secrecy, misrepresentation, and indifference. And yet the present view is that too much market knowledge could cause a panic and a run by Australian holders of toxic assets. The consequence would be a fall in the price of shares as funds liquidated their portfolios on behalf of shareholders wanting to exercise their cash options.

Continuing ignorance means that most Australians don't know how much of their compulsory superannuation they have lost — nor even what the investments were that they lost money on. They have no idea of the comparative performance of the multitude of superannuation funds in Australia.

This problem harks back to the old accountancy trick that is discussed elsewhere in this book in regard to transfer pricing. The losses in the superannuation funds will only crystallise when they are taken up in the annual returns of the funds. When that happens, a lot of people may be very upset. The obvious strategy for the funds is to delay disclosure until the situation improves. This may, of course, result in further losses. In the meantime, we have not had the information necessary to make an informed decision about the investments of our superannuation funds.

The funds are putting a spin on the situation and saying that, in the long run, you will get your money back. But what happens if you want to retire soon? Most of the larger contributors are older, and will never get all their money back. The truth is that this is a disingenuous view of an acceptable use of capital. Who would willingly accept a return of 0 per cent after three years?

This is not sensible management by the government. By allowing the superannuation industry to create its own rules about disclosure of loss for its own benefit, both the government and the industry are relying on popular ignorance to keep investors pacified while they are losing their savings or receiving no return on their capital.

***

The fundamental tenet of free-market economics is also its fundamental flaw. It relies upon a hypothesis developed in the 1970s by two American economists, Thomas Sargent and Robert Lucas, whose core theory is that each individual always acts in his/her own best interest, and that this is rational. Therefore the sum of all actions and decisions by all individuals has to be a rational and optimal set of actions and decisions that require no intervention by government. Individuals in a society, in total, always have perfect knowledge of the market.

This theory was embraced by the Reserve Bank of Australia in the 1990s when it decided that it had no function to perform in the economy, other than to manage inflation through interest-rate corrections.

It has certainly been embraced by the Productivity Commission, which sees its role as removing government interventions that take the form of regulation of industries. For example, Gary Banks, the chairman of the commission, has railed against the creation of major government initiatives in relation to climate change, on the basis that this intervention will create a new opportunity for rent-seekers attempting to obtain government assistance at the expense of other industries.

Of course, the rational behaviourists didn't bother to check empirically whether their theory was borne out in practice. This was just as well for them, as the facts don't fit the theory, and never have.

First, the fact is that there are many poor, ignorant, uneducated, lazy, and addicted people who gamble, drink, smoke, drive dangerously, and take too much medication. Many of their actions may not be rational most of the time. Most of us would admit, if pressed, that we act irrationally part of the time.

Second, few people are intimate with econometric modelling. The presence of the Greek letters for sigma and delta, and a time series from n to 1 in an equation, loses most readers. Most of the equations are limited by assumptions that make their solution easy and their relevance to reality negligible. In fact, there are very few situations in the market place that can be accurately predicted by models — and they don't include guessing the rate of future economic growth, the level of unemployment, stock-market prices, or even the names of winning racehorses. It would be instructive to test particular predictions after the event to see how often they are incorrect. As we have seen, part of the institutional buying of collateralised debt obligations was based on mathematical models which assumed that house foreclosures would result, in aggregate, in auctions where at least the mortgage loan amount would be recovered. They haven't come close.

The global financial disaster has been akin to the chain reaction that causes a nuclear explosion. No single foreclosure would have created a problem; for that matter, probably tens of thousands of foreclosures wouldn't have mattered. The crisis occurred because so many foreclosures resulted from an endemic lack of integrity in the disclosure and mortgage-decision process, and the subsequent passing on of the risk to financial institutions that were unaware of the true extent of the risk in the first place.

This result will be played out in class actions all over the world for the next 20 years.

The making of major assumptions, without engaging in empirical testing in the market, is common in mathematical and econometric models. Their construction and use is completely unlike what happens during the development of a major new pharmaceutical drug, when the candidate product is tested to empirical exhaustion over a 12-year period. The researchers don't rely on assumptions about the drug's attributes or on models of its potential effects, because a global product that doesn't work in the real world can cost the drug company billions of dollars in a resultant class action. Coming up with an efficacious and harmless drug for even 98 per cent of the population isn't good enough.

The fate of Dow Corning's silicone-based breast-implants is an example of what can go wrong for consumers and corporations if insufficient testing is done. After a horrendous litany of adverse physical effects was revealed, the resultant global class action cost Dow Corning and other pharmaceutical companies more than $10 billion over 15 years.

By comparison, the level of mathematics employed in economics is simplistic. Mathematicians and actuaries are not economists.

Ken Henry, secretary of the Treasury, has been a trenchant champion of the veracity of Treasury projections. The facts are that Henry has been at Treasury for a long time, and was certainly there as a very senior Treasury officer during the previous ten years. Why hadn't Treasury modelled the potential risk of a global financial disaster? Some of the many risk models used by the institutions that bought the collateralised debt obligations included over 100,000 risk scenarios. The disaster somehow didn't fit into these top 100,000 possibilities.

The Rudd government should ask Treasury to undertake an analysis of its surplus-and-deficit predictions, and compare them with what actually happened over, say, the past decade; or compare what was modelled to what happened to the Australian economy in times of volatility during the 1970s, 1980s, and 1990s. The Treasury secretary's heavy-handed responses to any criticism of Treasury projections is the sort of elitist, omniscient nonsense that sounds funny, but doesn't really address the problem at hand. We need to get over admiring the Keatingesque insult, and instead do some real work that shows us whether or not Treasury has been, in the past, relatively accurate with its forecasts.

Finally, the self-interest of the sellers of low-doc mortgages led to them illegally concealing information from the mortgagees and the purchasers of the bundled collateralised debt obligations. The purchasers then concealed the value composition and character of the various securities supporting the CDO. So much for 'perfect market knowledge'.

The low-doc purveyors sought no documents to justify a statement of income and assets (so they became so-called 'liar loans'), and in some cases multiplied the mortgagee's income three or more times to justify the arithmetic for repayment of the loan.

Why didn't the prudential processes of the major financial institutions pick this up? These events occurred from 2003 to 2007, when all of a sudden the ballooning foreclosure rate made the commercial paper market so leery that the banking system froze in a few weeks. This was no overnight phenomenon.

It should be obvious that the intellectual foundations of free-market economics had no impact on the market behaviour of numerous powerful individuals and companies that committed major crimes against millions of people. We are still to witness the full financial and social impact of those crimes, as those with marginal loans or those recently unemployed are drawn into the financial whirlpool. We are still to see the class-action litigation unfold.

The only thing that would save some of the financial-sector offenders is a level of government intervention costing trillions of dollars. And how would the underlying economic theory survive that catastrophe? How can anyone argue with a straight face that free-market economics is still some eternal economic truth?

It will be interesting to look back in ten years' time, when the class actions are in full swing, and see who the defendants are. The show won't only be on in America.

Chapter Eight
Fixing the Problem: domestic strategies

The reaction of government and many public-service mandarins to the global financial disaster is partially based on denial. This attitude makes some pragmatic sense, as they and all of us want to avoid setting off a panic.

Ironically, until recently most of the senior public servants in the economic departments and statutory authorities were all true believers in free-market economics. There are still some stone-warrior recidivists among them now. This school of believers want the chips to fall where they may, to let the next group of self-interested shysters start to develop the latest elixir for immortal life or perhaps university courses in alchemy. The alchemists may be the new economists. Their new economy will sit on the ruins of the old.

This may sound extreme, but readers should understand that, for the past 20 years at least, there was no place in any major government economic forum or institution for someone who believed that the government had to be involved in regulation of the economy. This wasn't an open environment where clever, experienced people could hold an alternative view.

Some people, inside and outside the technostructure, take the view that nothing serious has happened because they are not personally affected. This perspective is generally limited to childless white males, less than 35 years old, working in the services or professional sectors, or in the middle reaches of think tanks and the public service, who are receiving high incomes. They have no concept of the capital outlays on houses, children, travelling expenses, and miscellaneous costs that await them, and have not modelled those projections. Perhaps they expect to inherit the money they will need.

Alternatively, if they are receiving high levels of income, and sold shares on margin, they may have made a fortune during the downturn. They are also benefiting from historically low interest rates.

We have an imperfect knowledge of the damage caused by the global financial disaster, and we will not be told the full story.

It was instructive to watch the US congressional hearings in 2009, during which congressman Alan Grayson questioned the chairman of the US Federal Reserve, Ben Bernanke, and other senior officers (including the inspector-general) about the $553 billion that the Fed had lent to central banks all over the world. The central banks then on-lent the money in their own countries to banks, companies, and other organisations that the Fed can't or won't reveal.

Even New Zealand got $US9 billion. What did they do with that money? How much money did Australia get from the Federal Reserve? How much has the Reserve Bank of Australia lent to domestic banks?

We have no process available to us with which to publicly question the Reserve Bank or Treasury on these matters. We have no parliamentary process to discover the truth — other than rigged royal commissions that flow from investigative processes which were anachronisms 50 years ago.

Why doesn't the government use its powers to force major enterprises and government institutions to disclose the full extent of our exposure and the timing of its realisation?

Some companies have done so to a limited extent because they simply cannot meet their debt-payment commitments in the next few years, and they accept that they have disclosure obligations to the market as public companies. These are the companies that are repairing their balance sheets. There is a deafening silence from those that are not in this position.

In Australia, there has been no government or media pressure on the banks, the Future Fund, the financial institutions, the regulatory authorities, or the superannuation funds to disclose their losses.

The problem with not knowing the full extent of the disaster is that sensible (even rational) people simply have no idea about how to react. Anyone who looks at the sub-prime mortgage figures and capital raisings has to conclude that a lot of the iceberg is still submerged.

Inevitably, the number of loss disclosures will increase, and the particular tranches of CDO securities that were parcelled up and sold in Australia will be revealed.

In the US, 500,000 people a month were retrenched in 2007–08. Between the onset of the recession in December 2007 and December 2009, about 7.2 million Americans lost their jobs. Although the monthly job-loss rate has since fallen, the total of unemployed workers is still increasing, bringing more and more people into the vortex of the jobless whirlpool. There is certainly no suggestion that the employment rate in the US is increasing.

It is logical that as the aggregate level of unemployment increases, the rate of unemployment growth will slow. It will not continue at the breakneck speed of the early days — or no one will be employed. What is needed to break the cycle is employment growth.

So what should Australia do to meet the challenge? Spending government money, ignoring everything except the blatant disasters that can't be diminished by any amount of spin, and talking up the economy is not a long-term package of initiatives that will solve the problem.

My strategy to fix Australia's problems created by the global financial disaster can be divided into two quite separate initiatives that do not involve stimulus packages or media spin. They do involve major shifts in attitude from those that have been rusted on over 40 years, and a great deal of hard work. Our greatest problem will be to move past the free-market orthodoxy that has shaped the minds and careers of many powerful people in the public service, and of many senior advisers to government, academic economists, and senior media people.

There are a number of changes that need to be made to our own economy which would reverse the long process of policy neglect that was actively promoted by free-market advocates. These are discussed below.

The next chapter deals with doing what the free-market economists long advocated but never did. It involves internationalising the Australian economy — creating an outward-looking, international perspective, and being internationally competitive. We have to take from the major economies those policies that have put them in the major league. They don't ship out raw materials for overseas value-adding. They do create non-tariff barriers to defend their industries. They do create a balanced economy that stands on the pillars of manufacturing, agriculture, finance, and services.

It is almost embarrassing to remember the extent of the lionisation of the Australian services sector. My experience overseas is that people are puzzled by the way we have treated our huge, rich country with contempt, and focused instead on economic activities (such as financing and logistics) that are, generally, a simple by-product of the major activity of adding value to our abundant resources. They are also amazed that we have managed to sell so much of our heritage to support the importation of products we could make for ourselves.

Solution #1: Find out the size of the loss and who the losers are

The denial and obfuscation that is happening now will delay the creation of policies needed to redress the situation. Yet we have a right to know what we have lost and what we are likely to lose if we do not change our investments or our superannuation fund. The banks and the funds know exactly what their remaining exposure is—and that exposure flows through directly to those who have money invested with them.

If we take a leaf out of the free-market bible, the first strategy required to fix the Australian problem is to obtain perfect knowledge about at least one aspect of the disaster.

How much have we lost? What can be recovered?

We need to know how much investment there has been in toxic loans and other CDOs that are still held by banks, superannuation funds, investment funds, the Future Fund, and anyone else. The total investment by local government may be known already, as many councils are trying to start a class action against the loan promoters. The word on the street is that, collectively, the councils have invested more than $4 billion of their ratepayers' funds in these arcane, high-risk overseas instruments. The first number publicly quoted was a lot lower—$700 million—but what is the real number? Many councils have refused to participate in the class action, presumably to avoid having to own up to the size of their likely losses.

Superannuation funds are subject to the reporting requirements of the Australian Prudential Regulation Authority, so they are subject to mandatory disclosure. They compete with each other to establish superior performance-levels, so it is likely that there have been winners and losers in the investment race that ought to be called the Collateralised Debt Obligation Stakes.

Those who missed out on the CDO offerings are now the winners. We know that our superannuation funds managed a trillion dollars until recently, and that this total was increasing by $90 billion a year. At one stage, the speculators' theory was that the stock market had to keep rising because it was being driven by the massive inflow of superannuation funds. Where will they invest now? Will they just go straight back into a share market littered with the financial equivalent of land mines? It would be severely career-limiting for a fund investment manager to have invested in Asciano, ABC, Allco, Babcock & Brown, Storm, Macquarie (still 50 per cent down from its expensive peak), or Virgin, or any of the property trusts that collectively announced profit write-downs of $13 billion for 2008–09. Those still employed must be sitting in their offices, waiting either for miracles or their pink slips.

State government infrastructure authorities were once significant overseas investors of their surplus funds. They lost a lot of money in the 1980s when they punted on foreign-exchange hedging derivatives, borrowing money in foreign currencies to do so. Those who made the loans departed quickly from the infrastructure authorities.

In the early 1980s, a story appeared in the *Business Review Weekly* magazine about a year after the Australian dollar had been trading at around 50 cents to the US dollar. The new financial gurus of the instrumentalities were being hailed by the *BRW* as heroes, just because the Australian dollar had risen to about 80 cents to the US dollar and thereby repaid a part of the authorities' losses.

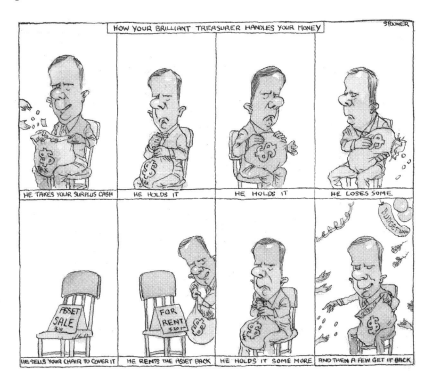

151

The gurus' choice had been very simple: the new players could realise their losses and join their predecessors in some form of alternative employment, or simply go to the beach, do nothing, and hope. I wonder where their excess funds have been invested in the past few years.

In the present crisis, the banks are the largest potential losers. They have borrowed our private foreign debt of $700 billion and are also borrowing to meet business-lending requirements. They have already raised $100 billion behind the shield of the government's 100 per cent guarantee. Who lent them the $100 billion? The investment funds they receive are usually 90-day and 180-day bills sourced from wholesale funds that extinguish the line of credit at the end of the period—at which time there is no guarantee that the fund will reinvest in Australian equities. These funds are part of the market for commercial paper that froze and nearly brought the global economy to an end.

Why, if our banks are so strong, have they had to borrow such a large amount of money?

Another problem for the banks is not their own holdings of toxic loans, but the financial state of their lenders. They may not have any money left to lend, or they may be desperate to recover what they have already lent.

In both these cases (and for the Future Fund), the federal and state governments have the power or moral suasion necessary to force disclosure. The question is whether they have the courage to do so. There is little doubt that disclosure would change the public perception of the various institutions, and that it would result in gains and losses of business for the banks.

There is a case for non-disclosure, but the cost is too high. In order to protect the interests of the institutions, companies, and funds, we would have to ignore the interests of Australians who have invested their savings and their superannuation in these enterprises. The government transferred $60 billion of its surplus to the Future Fund to shore up the Commonwealth superannuation deficiencies, which had been growing for decades (so much for the quality of actuarial advice). No one told us about that debacle and the consequential liability it imposed upon the Australian people. This works out at about $3000 per man, woman, and child in Australia, but apparently wasn't worthy of investigation.

A lot of people don't want to know. It is too depressing. The fact is that ignorance will only increase the losses as more loans become toxic. You can't stop this process unless you know whether the losses have stopped by themselves (that is, whether the toxic loans and other debts have been flushed out of the enterprises' portfolios), or you have to move whatever capital is left.

Solution #2: Get Australia's accounts in order, and live within our means

Australians (through their banks) owe the rest of the world a lot of money. The government doesn't owe it (or at least it didn't, until it undertook its stimulus-response measures to the global financial crisis); we do.

The Australian current-account deficit (CAD) is a simple balance sheet that contains two categories of income received and expenditure incurred by the private sector.

The first category in the CAD balance sheet is what is called 'merchandise trade'. This consists of physical goods, such as machinery and other capital equipment, cars, shoes, computers, clothes, electrical goods, and everything else that we consume, use in our homes and buildings, live in, wear, or use to make or grow goods in Australia.

The second category is non-physical. It consists of services, intellectual property, royalties, dividends, interest, investments, pensions, and debt payments.

ANNUAL INCOME TWENTY POUNDS, ANNUAL EXPENDITURE NINETEEN NINETEEN SIX, RESULT HAPPINESS. ANNUAL INCOME TWENTY POUNDS, ANNUAL EXPENDITURE TWENTY POUNDS OUGHT AND SIX, RESULT MISERY."(MR. MICAWBER IN DAVID COPPERFIELD)

Both categories involve exports to the rest of the world, for which we receive income or other revenue; and imports from the rest of the world of goods or services, or any other intangibles that we have purchased, which we have to pay for.

For a real-world demonstration, I have used data provided by the Reserve Bank of Australia to construct an example, based on export and import headings employed by the bank, to calculate a representative account of Australia's monthly import debits and export credits, and the resulting nett balance of that account:

How to create a current-account deficit [in $millions]

Merchandise Trade

Exports

Rural	Non-Rural		Total
$1000	$3000		$4000

Imports

Consumption	Capital	Intermediate	Total
$3000	$1000	$1000	$5000

Balance on merchandise trade ($1000)

Trade in Interest, Income, and Intellectual Property

Nett services	Nett income		Total
($500)	($300)		($800)

Current-account balance ($1800)

According to the Reserve Bank's statistical series, Australia's current account has been negative every quarter of every year since the June quarter of 1973. That is, in every quarter since 1973, we have paid out more for imports of goods and services than we have been paid for our exports.

This invariable deficit has created a foreign debt now approaching $700 billion. This debt is funded either by us borrowing from overseas, or by selling Australian property, businesses, and assets to overseas interests.

The global financial crisis has created a massive problem for us if we maintain our appetite for foreign debt and try to keep living off the sale of our assets and resources.

Those who lent us the money in better days or bought our assets may now have very substantial liquidity problems of their own, or they may have other global opportunities that are more attractive than those offered by Australian assets. They may want their money back. Or they may want to sell their property or business.

Many of the loans are in the form of short-term financial instruments — in which case, should the call be made, we would not be given further time to make the repayments. The question is whether the Australian government can continue to guarantee the banks, and whether it will be willing to take the steps of virtually nationalising any banks that are ultimately found to be insolvent.

China has the world's largest current-account surplus: in 2008, it was $US426 billion; Japan's surplus was $177 billion, down one-third on its 2007 figure. It ought to be salutary for our policy-makers to see that Japan, which has a vigorous industry-policy culture and a protectionist stance, keeps churning out trade surpluses, decade after decade.

THE BRAVE FREE TRADER

The US has the world's largest current-account deficit — $US664 billion in 2008. However, I don't believe this figure is a genuine problem, as America owns most of the global brands, and its global assets would be worth tens of trillions of dollars. American multinationals are undoubtedly owed further trillions by their wholly owned affiliates all over the world.

Ideally, the raw current-account balances for each country should be deflated by an index based on the size of the national incomes of each country. This would create a better measurement of the significance of both the current-account balances over time and the total amount of the foreign debt.

Globally, Australia ranks almost last in the current-account-balance hierarchy. Our current-account deficit in 2006–07 was $59.2 billion. Our total foreign-debt liabilities totalled $972 billion in the same year. We have offsetting assets of $428 billion, leaving us with a nett foreign debt of $544 billion. About $100 billion of the assets are owned by our government, so our nett private debt was almost $650 billion in 2006–07. It is now over $700 billion.

We have neither the depth nor range of assets, the retained earnings overseas, the investments in technology demonstrated by the US, nor the currency strategy and assets of the Japanese and the Chinese. We are simply spending too much on imports, and exporting virtually no value-added products.

Our gross foreign-debt liability of close to a trillion dollars is a real problem. We don't know who our creditors are, or their present financial positions. We don't know if our debts are payable within six months or six years.

For the past 20 years, an army of academic and media apologists has variously said that our rising foreign debt is only a temporary problem because we are incurring it to buy capital equipment that will increase our exports of elaborately transformed manufactures (which hasn't happened), or that the Australian dollar exchange-rate will adjust to slow the inflow of imports and increase the outflow of exports (which also hasn't happened).

Treasury secretary Ken Henry has developed the latest excuse for a continuing CAD. He believes that the massive investment needed to develop our mineral and fuel resources can only be met from overseas. This idea assumes that the government shouldn't (and won't) do what other countries have done: borrow the money. It could then pay it back from the proceeds of royalties and specific industry taxes.

The other and more likely alternative is that we will, as most underdeveloped countries do, sell off the rest to the global miners and fuel companies. In both cases, the CAD may or may not grow, depending upon the extent to which the revenue stream from the taxation of such exports offsets the new debt payments or the use of the sales proceeds by the present owners.

Instead, we are starting to look like a 21st-century Argentina. Our resources are huge, but we do not process them. We are bringing in more and more guest workers and students to do the menial tasks. Argentina imported Irish navvies in the late-19th century for the same kind of labouring and construction jobs.

It would be interesting to discover just how much Australian property and business is in the hands of the 10,000 multinational subsidiaries resident in Australia. We have been selling the farm to all comers for a long time now.

Our current-account deficit and our foreign debt lack the

redeeming features of the debts carried by the US and the Europeans. We are not global citizens who influence and own assets and property in any market that we may enter. We are not significant exporters of goods and services. We are doing well with our quarrying activities, but every quarry is ultimately an abandoned hole.

The US and the Europeans have dominated global trade through their multinational companies. They have the ability to retain money in the form of loans all over the world, and to avoid repatriating it to the home country where they would have to pay tax. This explains the 3 per cent tax rate quoted by President Obama for the 100-largest US companies.

The Chinese and the Japanese have pursued a slightly different strategy. They have invested any current-account surpluses they have in American and other foreign equities and companies. This has created a major furore in the US, but is really no different from the US investment in Australia.

There is not much point in accumulating currency. It is much better for foreign companies and sovereign funds to own resources, properties, and businesses, especially if there is no chance of the local government ever nationalising the foreign assets.

Very few Australian companies have significant networks of affiliates operating in foreign jurisdictions. In those rare cases where we do have the ability to create global products, the trend has been to base the head offices offshore. This move is generally justified by the availability of taxation incentives and access to more capital at better interest rates.

We are at the bottom of the list of trading nations because our policies and our continual surplus of consumer-product imports have placed us there. This can't be explained as some clever global strategy or subtle economic theory. Our position is a consequence of our failure to add value to our resources and to create industries that can dominate our local markets. The global bailout of the financial markets demonstrates that the services sector might not have its hand out often; but when it does, the cost to the community dwarfs anything ever given to the manufacturing sector.

A final major problem is that a large part of the current-account deficit and foreign debt arises from transfer-pricing practices by multinationals located in our economy. Many multinational parent companies overcharge their affiliates for products, and for intellectual property and services. What do these overcharges mean? Are they ever paid, or are they simply devices aimed at minimising tax obligations that are often not met or settled for a much smaller amount when the ATO finally audits the affiliate?

What those overcharges do is overstate the value of merchandise imports, as well as imported intangibles and intellectual property. They create debts on which interest is charged and paid, which in turn attracts a withholding tax that is much lower than the company tax rate, and which in any case is only paid when the fee for imported intangibles and intellectual property is remitted. We not only miss out on the company tax, but we are creating a major segment of Australian business that never makes a profit because the overseas parents have found better things to do with the profits than pay Australian company tax on them.

Identifying illicit transfer pricing by multinationals is not just about collecting some tax that should have been paid, and then imposing late-payment interest and penalties. In itself, this is a valuable addition to federal government revenue, but it is a once-off payment.

The real issue is that excessive transfer prices reduce income that is declared in Australia, and they increase the income paid overseas. For example, an additional tax collection of $3 billion means that Australian income had previously been understated by $10 billion. These numbers are about the magnitude of additional tax collections in the period from 1990 to 2000 that were paid by multinationals as a consequence of the ATO's transfer-pricing tracking program. They are a fraction of the additional tax paid and the income earned in Australia following the ATO's audit and settlements.

A long-term and substantial benefit to the nation that accrues from the programme comes from the annual additions to multinational affiliate income that then flow through to our gross national income.

Of the approximately 10,000 multinational affiliates in Australia, we have no public knowledge of the extent of their ownership of Australian assets, the level of their indebtedness to their parent company, or the aggregate income that they are generating each year. They obviously constitute a very substantial part of the Australian economy.

The Australian Taxation Office has managed to effectively review only about 500 of these 10,000 companies since 1992. Admittedly, those reviewed include most of the very large multinationals. I appreciate the severe difficulties that are involved in completing complex audit processes — the average transfer-pricing review takes 28 months, and in some cases the process takes five or more years and involves government-to-government negotiations. Audits usually last longer; some may take ten or more years to complete.

The government should follow the precedent it set with

the Industries Commission in the 1980s, when it established a limit of 12 months for the organisation to conduct an inquiry and submit its report. This then forced the commission to set up a strict timetable, and forced the industry it was dealing with to meet specific but not impossible deadlines. Before then, the commission would take up to seven years to complete a major inquiry.

I believe that two years is a sufficient time to complete a transfer-pricing review or audit, provided that the ATO is allowed to use its resources properly and that it insists upon company responses within a reasonable time.

The transfer-pricing programme is a relatively easy way to start to reverse the current-account deficit and to ensure that multinational firms resident in Australia pay their fair share of tax. Obviously, if they don't, they obtain a very substantial competitive advantage over their Australian competitors.

It should be possible to complete an outcome-assessment total for the ATO's transfer-pricing programme that shows how much revenue has been received in additional tax, late payment interest, and penalties. This estimate should include a calculation of the general magnitude of future income that will be derived for Australia as a consequence of agreements reached between the ATO and companies about the amount of income that would be earned by the Australian affiliates of multinational companies if they were to adopt a genuine arms' length standard.

Assuming that the company tax rate is 30 per cent, it would be very surprising if the programme hasn't already added at least $10 billion a year to Australia's national income. This would have constituted a total deduction of $150 billion from the current-account deficit over the past 15 years, which is about how long the ATO programme has been operating. There would be substantial future gains available to the nation by applying this obvious method of housekeeping. All it requires is the will to initiate the programme on a much wider scale than has occurred until now, and to complete it in a sensible time frame.

Solution #3: Reconstruct the knowledge base of the Australian economy

Employment loss in the federal and state public services is not an inevitable consequence of introducing innovations that increase productivity. We are nowhere near the point where we know enough about the characteristics of our industries and markets. Our knowledge base has been eroded during the past 30 years by the view that government scrutiny was a form of intervention in free markets.

In 15 years, our attitude towards older working Australians and part-time work have changed so much that the retirement-age ethos has moved from employees being able to leave the workforce with a retirement package at the age of 55, to them being ineligible for a pension, to most working into their mid-60s or even later. The number of part-time workers in the economy has increased by two million in the same period.

The change has been driven by an ageing population, more women in the workforce, fewer full-time (and very few life-time) jobs, and a much more relaxed attitude towards having a career with a number of employers.

This shift has not generally been transmitted to the public sector. Public servants and government employees are full time, and have a job for life if they want it. The public service generally makes no attempt to accelerate projects by manning up for major projects when they occur. The time-line for completion by existing staff just gets longer.

Boeing, which is the US's largest exporter, no longer offers any full-time career opportunities. It has adopted a contract approach for particular projects. This move by Boeing, which is a global company whose major asset is its engineering intellectual property, shows how much the employment paradigm has shifted in the past 20 years. Even a company with a global engineering advantage is prepared to put at risk the intangible assets of its workers' knowlege and skills by shifting to project-based employment.

There is obviously greater uncertainty and complexity for individuals who are obliged to approach employment on a part-time or project-by-project basis. But beggars can't be choosers. If, during a second-wave downturn during the global financial disaster, we reach an unemployment level approaching 10 per cent, a lot of those unemployed would prefer some employment to none at all.

The great difference between now and the Depression is that many of the newly unemployed will be in the services sector. They have education and aptitude, and could be employed in national projects such as building a new national industry database to replace the degraded and outdated information we now possess.

A national industry and business census would be a good starting-point to determine just what our economic assets are. Similarly, we need to measure the extent of the change in importing patterns since the introduction of online purchasing from offshore (using Amazon, eBay, and others), and the generous value threshold that has been granted of $1000 before duty and GST is collected. Customs and the ABS don't want to measure this, because it would create extra work for them when they are concentrating on border security (in the case of Customs), or withdrawing from major imports data-collection and analysis (in the case of the ABS).

PETER COSTELLO, VICTIM OF CHRONIC NARCISSISM, HOUNDED BY INSENSITIVE MEDIA FLATTERY, SLYLY BASKS IN THE GENIAL INDIFFERENCE TO HIS $62 000 000 000 CURRENT ACCOUNT DEFICIT

PETRA CASTILLO, VICTIM OF CHRONIC ASTHMA AND BACK PAIN FROM YEARS OF CASUAL LOW-PAID CLEANING, APPLIES FOR ANOTHER JOB BEFORE HER CHILDREN COME HOME FROM AN UNDERFUNDED SCHOOL

One of the great achievements of the United States during the Depression years was its creation of the Tennessee Valley Authority (TVA) by the then president, Franklin Delano Roosevelt. The TVA Act passed through Congress on 18 May 1933. It was, in the words of the president, 'a corporation clothed with the involvement power of government but possessed in its creation of the flexibility and initiative and management of a private enterprise'.

The focus of the TVA was on the rural sector of the United States. It taught new farming methods to farmers, built dams, and became the largest public power-provider in the States.

The TVA has continued to create major infrastructure in the US for the past 75 years. We could learn from its example, and broaden the TVA concept to create an Australian 21st-century public corporation that develops our knowledge of our industry resources and their ownership. It could measure the quantity and analyse the detail of our international trade, examine the cost and pricing structures of our imports and exports of goods and services, and identify the opportunities for meaningful innovation and productivity gains.

This massive research-and-knowledge acquisition task cannot be achieved within the infrastructure of government departments and authorities. It demands a fresh analytical approach, a new economic perspective, and an ability to override the resistance of traditional public-service entities. There will never be a better time to start a knowledge revolution.

We can either pay people to be idle, or to perform an invaluable task in the interests of Australia. Our knowledge base has been eroded by an entrenched conviction that government should not intrude in the business of business. We need to begin again from an unbiased perspective.

There should be no boundaries to the government's knowledge of the economy. Much of the damage done by the global financial disaster took place before governments were aware that the financial sector had created processes that were beyond conventional risk-management. No government regulatory body warned any government that the disaster was about to occur or was in progress.

When we have this knowledge, there is nothing to prevent the government from getting the best businesspeople in the country to try to create national projects. Now is the time to stop rubbishing the government and insisting that it stay out of the market and industry. We need to re-discover our national pride and purpose.

Whipped on by the financial sector, and its urgers and acolytes, we have come to adopt the attitude that our farmers and manufacturers are second rate. As a result, we have spent the last 30 years selling our farms and annihilating our manufacturing base. Yet we are a nation that must ultimately rely upon what it grows and makes.

Now is the time to try to buy back the farms and regenerate manufacturing. This was honest Rex Connor's good idea 35 years ago, and he was ridiculed for it. A lot of the overseas owners of Australian businesses are now sellers. We should join the smarties who are now snapping them up cheaply.

Solution #4: Review all government expenditure, employment, and outsourcing

'Innovation' and 'productivity improvements' are the buzzwords of the Rudd government. In practice, the only way to gain such improvements in organisations that basically provide government services is to reduce their head count. And yet, from 2002 to 2008, employment by the Commonwealth government, state governments, councils, and statutory authorities grew from 1.5 million to 1.75 million people.

It is now almost a decade since Osama Bin Laden's 11 September attack on the World Trade Center. Since that time, Australia's defence and security forces have grown enormously. The Defence budget increased from $12.6 billion in 2001 to $26.7 billion in 2008–9. Customs has forgotten about trade facilitation, and now focuses on border security: its staffing has grown from 3900 to 5450 people, and its budget has almost doubled. The Australian Federal Police has increased its staff from 4200 to 6000.

The latest federal turf war has been a pitched battle over who has primary responsibility for border security. Six departments — Foreign Affairs and Trade; Prime Minister and Cabinet; Industry; Defence; Transport and Infrastructure; and the Australian Customs Service — have been involved in fighting over this growth opportunity.

Empire building has always been a preoccupation of the public service. Privatisation and outsourcing has been an off-balance sheet way of growing the bureaucratic empires, but the people involved stay the same: the private consultants and senior management in the new authorities are usually ex-public servants.

State forces such as the police have also gained enormously from the security mania. The cost of staging APEC in Sydney, for example, was horrendous. Against the backdrop of the entire city being emptied, a solitary car crossed the Harbour Bridge on the Saturday of the APEC leaders' conference, and a two-metre-high steel barrier was erected for three kilometres along Pitt Street.

I was in a meeting room with a client on about the twentieth floor of the Hyatt hotel on Hyde Park during the APEC meeting in 2007, when a helicopter came within ten metres of the picture window where we were sitting — I assume because the pilot enjoyed frightening a few men in suits. And yet the ABC comedy team The Chaser was able to sail through the security and to make fools of the police.

The expansion of the public service is only a part of the costs of our obsession with our public safety. Our bodies are screened, our bags are screened, we take off our shoes and belts—and this is only the security process that we see. There are probably still armed marshals on flights. We eat in food halls where we are not allowed to put scraps and packaging in the garbage bins.

What events since 11 September justify this costly vigilance? We are told about thwarted threats, and watch trials of people who have talked about attacks. Some attacks have occurred, but are they any more frequent than the attacks in the 1970s, 1980s, and 1990s?

There have always been fanatics in industrialised societies. The Weathermen, the Baader-Meinhof gang, and the Symbionese Liberation Army are just a few. We need to be protected from them, but we don't need to be protected from us. The size of the response and its spread suggests that this is really about creating power and income, rather than about protecting society. Security is not negotiable, and both the private and public sectors are paying billions of dollars a year for it. You can't joke about security at an airline terminal.

From 2000–01 to 2008–09, the Australian public-service payroll grew from 213,000 to 250,000 people. Prime Minister Rudd is now publicly addressing the need to review public-service growth using the same numbers. There has also been an explosion in tasks outsourced to consultants. It would be interesting to know how much the private-consultancy bill has grown for both the federal and state governments, but this number is almost impossible to calculate. Senate Order No. 9 requires federal government bodies to disclose any consultancies they award that are worth over $100,000, but finding and aggregating the amount is a massive job. In any case, there is no similar requirement for disclosure by the state governments.

The calculation of public-service employment numbers has also been complicated by the growth in the number of privatised authorities in all three levels of government. What has certainly happened has been an explosion in the income levels of senior personnel in privatised authorities.

The major beneficiaries have not been the people of Australia, but the government bodies and the contractors who have massively ramped up the national expenditure on defence and security.

In the same period, there has been a huge increase in the privatisation of government infrastructure, the provision of IT, security and other consultancy services, and outsourcing and offshoring. There is no single, simple source of information about the growth of public-sector employment and its total cost. There should be.

There is a national necessity to review the size of the public service and the defence forces. The same opportunity exists with councils and state government departments. Why are their council and state government employees' jobs sacrosanct? There is duplication and hidden overemployment in the public service and the councils.

Without doubt, the privatisations that took place in the 1980s and 1990s, and the employment changes generated by information-technology systems, reduced the size of the various public services considerably. But that reduction has since been reversed, and public-service employment is now ballooning — along with the external payments and indirect employment by governments.

The danger of a government-awarded consultancy is that it is simply an expensive way for a department to be told what it wants to hear. There is no real audit of advice or any protocol in place to prevent former senior public servants — or, for that matter, ex-senior politicians — from providing consultancy services to their former colleagues and present friends. It is an open secret that you cannot see a minister in federal or state governments unless the door is opened by a former parliamentary colleague or a past party luminary. This is probably not the case for captains of industry, but they have a separate power-base.

This process gets worse as a government becomes entrenched after a few terms in office. First-time governments are more accessible than re-elected governments. Governments that have been elected twice are basically inaccessible to all but the chosen ones.

Actual levels of service and information provided by government to the public seem to have declined and been obfuscated. The present disaster is an opportunity for the people to regain some control over management of the Australian public service.

We need to change the structure and business approach of the public sector, and redeploy many of the people who are performing tasks that should have been reshaped or eliminated long ago.

We need to look at consultancy payments, so we can decide if they are worthwhile. Some consultancies are charging daily rates to government that are comparable to the rates charged by the first-tier accountancy firms. The latter can charge these rates for what is only good, average service because they generally have a global brand name, access to massive professional-indemnity insurance, and resources in 150 countries that are used by all the affiliates of a multinational. From a quality standpoint, it is ludicrous for an accounting

partner to charge a daily rate higher than that of a senior
counsel of significant standing and reputation—but they do.

It is even more ludicrous for a local consultancy firm
without a brand name to charge the same rates as a first-tier,
international accountancy firm. At least the latter can be sued,
and have been, for providing inferior or incorrect advice. I
doubt that this has ever happened to a small, local consultant
working for government.

Hercules' task of cleaning the Augean stables to remove the
odour hanging over the Peloponnesus was simple compared to
the task of reforming the government sector.

The federal auditor-general does a good job with his
reviews of departments, but lacks sufficient resources. At the
political and bureaucratic level, the major elements of the
Commonwealth departmental review task are conducted by
the Department of Finance led by Lindsay Tanner.

In 2009, I watched Tanner address the National Press Club. He almost made me think that he was the very model of a modern major regulator. I really like the idea that the Rudd government is sweeping away fashionable economic assumptions. Some of its rhetoric — for instance, its commitment to creating evidence-based policy — has been balm for the soul. But we are yet to see the evidence.

The test for the minister for finance and deregulation is to demonstrate that his public-service razor is a scalpel professionally applied and honed by impartial research of the facts to improve the health of the economy. We have had enough of the old free-market razza matazz that hacks away at any government initiative or direction, and isn't overly worried by reality.

Tanner's acceptance of the idea that the core of the budget funds the cost of government, and that the balance pays for services and infrastructure for the Australian people, is a plain and commonsense premise, leading to a good conclusion.

The more we spend on government, the less we have available to spend on health, education, welfare, security infrastructure, and all the other government interventions in our society that are the purpose of government. As always, the real difficulty lies in how the philosophy is implemented. I know that the federal public service is quite capable of defending its own interests, and repelling razor gangs. Federal and state government departments are very used to turf wars.

Minister Tanner talked about reforms to property management, the use of frequent-flyer points, and the bulk-buying of transport services. These are good, little ideas, but they don't really touch the issues that should be addressed if the regulatory burden imposed by government on business is to be reformed — and the cost of government is to be reduced.

Nothing Lindsay Tanner said at the Press Club addressed the core need for regulatory reform. This lies in reforming the operational sectors of the government departments, where the great bulk of the staff, the power, and the costs reside.

As we have seen, very few people outside an operational area of the bureaucracy understand its specific tasks and responsibilities. And you simply can't reform what you don't understand.

We need to attack this knowledge deficiency. It is the great protective bulwark that prevents meaningful change.

In 1971, when I was (at the ripe old age of 24) the Inspector, Organisation in the Australian Customs Service in New South Wales, I would make submissions to the Commonwealth Public Service Board for new and upgraded positions. When public-service inspectors duly came over to negotiate the staffing changes, their starting position was that we had always asked for too much because we knew that they would cut us back. Their doubts about our requests were always right, but they lacked the functional knowledge of Customs activities to act on them in specific areas. We always relied upon the technicalities of the Customs functions to bamboozle the board.

Customs is still using antiquated port-clearance procedures that haven't changed in substance for over 50 years. We need to understand that this is wrong in principle. There are better, faster, and more cost-efficient ways readily available.

The regulatory Customs cost to small and medium-sized business is getting higher and higher. There was an attempt to change things several years ago with the Customs Trade Modernisation Act, but the cosmetic change that finally took place cost a billion dollars and achieved virtually nothing.

Lindsay Tanner's big picture is right. The more the government spends on itself, the less it has available to spend on services for the taxpayers. But getting into the big reduction-opportunities and past the bureaucratic barriers will take knowledge and action, as well as fine words. It will also require a level of objectivity that, at times, leaves behind the old allegiance to free-market economics.

The minister said: 'We can no longer afford to leave antiquated, overlapping contradictory regulation and haphazard policy in place.'

This is great stuff, but the Department of Finance is currently required to approve government-procurement contracts that are tendered for by local manufacturers in direct competition with importers from countries with which we have free-trade agreements. And guess what? Finance has a tendency to award close contests to the overseas tenderer, simply because it wants to be seen by other countries as being economically holier-than-thou.

Finance should start to do what its minister says it is doing. It needs to overhaul the operations of government, and to ignore the flummery of understandable but not crucial economies in administrative costs that miss the real opportunities of achieving substantial reductions in government spending. There are major operational areas of the public service whose staffing levels have remained untouched for a very long time.

This is not an easy task, and it will be opposed. The era of the global financial disaster may perhaps be the only time when public servants will have been frightened enough to sincerely contemplate change.

For example, Taxation, Treasury, Customs, Immigration, and the Australian Bureau of Statistics could all fit in one super department. The US has a Department of Homeland Security that amalgamated Immigration and Customs. Their territorial wars were fierce when it became obvious that there was only a need for one director of homeland security and that one of the old departmental directors had to drop back, change functions, or go. The same philosophy has merged Customs and Taxation in Holland, Canada, and a number of other countries.

This is not about sacking public servants. The goal should be to make their activities efficient, remove duplication and valueless activities, and find new, valuable functions to fill the available time. Re-acquainting themselves with businesses that make and provide goods would be a great starting point for some departments.

In the mind of Customs, 'the industry' it deals with comprises a small circle of Customs brokers, freight forwarders, and shipping companies. Customs can't seem to understand that service providers don't import or export anything. Customs only talks to importers and exporters if they employ brokers or ex-Customs officers.

Finally, we need to move away from the idea that Treasury supplies the only capable economic advisers to the government. They can't advise on defence, infrastructure, transfer pricing, transport, or industry. They have no relevant experience or knowledge of these areas.

The government and the public service should be working with people directly involved in industries and markets. Barriers have been created by associations and consultants that are really only serving their interests.

Solution #5: Involve people with empirical knowledge gained directly in industry

We need a different consultancy and collaborative process between government and industry. The present model favours public servants, business-association representatives, union officials, academics, and a few well-funded think tanks with an economic bias. If we are to reconstruct the Australian economy, we need to change the process of giving advice to government. This means including people other than those who only consult for or represent particular interest groups.

Some industry groups and other interests must, by necessity, be included because of the substance of their membership. It is important to try to avoid the ancient problem of simply selecting members who do nothing but pursue their own agenda and who have nothing to contribute on subjects beyond it.

This is particularly the case with employees of multi-nationals, their lawyers, and their chartered accountants, who want to be in government-appointed groups but are there only to serve their employers or clients, or to sell their services.

Solution #6: Stop talking about it and actually do something with COAG

The glacial pace of the reforms undertaken by the Council of Australian Governments (COAG) makes Treasury's modelling out to 2017 look like a short-term exercise.

COAG, whose membership includes all levels of government in Australia, including local government, has been meeting since May 1992. Admittedly, until recently, COAG was hampered by the endemic conflict between a group of state Labor governments and an entrenched and dismissive coalition government.

A lot of COAG's agreed policies are good, but they never get implemented. Its rate of policy implementation reminds me of the argument over the standardisation of state rail gauges, which went on between Victoria and New South Wales for 50 years, and forced travellers to change trains at Albury.

The policy-reform agenda includes national competition policy, water reform, research, counter-terrorism arrangements, environmental regulation, and the use of embryos in medical research. COAG's programme of reforms are — guess what? — major innovations. We can innovate right now by starting with these reforms and reinvigorating our economy. The mood for change is here.

It is instructive to observe the process of COAG on a matter as important as the National Reform Agenda (NRA). In June 2005, the Victorian premier outlined the imperative nature of the national reform of infrastructure and the skills-development system to meet the nation's future demands for a skilled workforce. From May to July 2006, the premier released more reports. In February 2007, the Productivity Commission released a report on the potential economic and fiscal impact of the NRA — its modelling found that the NRA could increase GDP by as much as 11 per cent after 25 years, which was even more heroic than the federal Treasury's modellers in the 2008–09 budget. In April 2007, the Victorian premier released three action plans outlining a ten-year vision.

Everyone agreed to the NRA, but the federal government wouldn't fund the reform proposals, even though it was awash with surpluses at that stage.

If every part of government is in COAG and they all agree to specific reforms, why don't they just do it? What is the status of the reforms now that the global crisis is here? Has COAG been overtaken by Infrastructure Australia, a new statutory body that formally reports to it?

COAG has constantly talked about major structural reform including infrastructure, but has never been able to get past pathetic squabbling about how much each party should pay towards the cost of the initiative. At least Infrastructure Australia has been voted a great deal of money by the federal government — $150 billion — and has a priority list for building infrastructure. The behaviour and procrastination of COAG is an indictment of our federal/state structure.

Chapter Nine
Fixing the Problem: international strategies

One relatively easy way for Australia to get its house in order is to end those policies and agreements that aren't working. A second but more difficult task is to introduce industry-policy measures similar to those that are working in Europe, the US, Japan, and Korea. The so-called free-trade agreements that Australia has entered into are demonstrably unfavourable to our interests; we should terminate them.

By using non-tariff barriers, all the major economies have managed the globalisation of their markets, and have ensured that their own manufacturing industries stay involved in processes that add value and generate employment. We need to stop being the one boy in the global band who thinks he is marching in step. Despite a great deal of self-congratulation in political circles and the media over our performance during the global financial crisis, the result has not come about through good management—it is a product of some good luck, some appropriate stimulus measures, and a lot of self-deception. We don't know how much damage has been done, because our governments have actively resisted finding out. So what are the likely solutions?

Solution #1: Jettison the toxic free-trade agreement with the US

The global financial disaster provides a pragmatic opportunity to jettison the US–Australia Free Trade Agreement (USAFTA). This, of course, presumes that we haven't been the unwitting beneficiary in the meantime of a multi-billion dollar handout from the Federal Reserve.

It is worth noting that Australia never pursued a free-trade agreement with the US until prime minister Howard and president Bush became firm friends.

President Barack Obama has promised to review the North American Free Trade Agreement (the agreement between the US, Canada, and Mexico), because he wants to be sure that any bilateral trade agreements are in America's interest.

The US Congress has used 'Buy American' legislation (which was first passed during the Great Depression) to protect America's steel industry, and this is likely to be extended to other major manufactured goods. There is no suggestion that Australia will be excluded from the steel-protection measures, even though our steel exports to the US are worth about half a billion dollars. Why aren't these measures deemed a major breach of the USAFTA? America terminated its free-trade agreement with Vietnam with less provocation.

Canadian companies are saying that Obama's 'Buy American' legislation is in breach of the North America free-trade agreement between the US, Canada, and Mexico.

The Productivity Commission has since been given a reference for a study into free-trade agreements, both bilateral and multilateral. It was given the reference on 23 December 2009, and it, in turn, only gave participants until 1 February 2010 to make submissions—while allowing itself 10 months to then write a study on a subject that has been very well understood for ages. I have the impression that the Minister for Trade, Simon Crean, who is an avid supporter of agreements, has been unhappy about the statistics coming out of the bilateral agreements. He should be—all of them show that Australia is being disadvantaged.

When the USAFTA commenced on 1 January 2005, it was promoted by then deputy prime minister and trade minister Mark Vaile as the most significant free-trade agreement in Australia's history. He said: 'This FTA is worth billions of dollars and will create thousands of jobs.'

The agreement followed a study by the Centre for International Economics (CIE), a private economic consultancy, undertaken for the Department of Foreign Affairs and Trade. The CIE study concluded: 'Over the first 20 years of the agreement the present values of the benefits to the Australian economy exceeds $57 billion, over 30,000 jobs will be created, and real wages will rise and all states and territories will be better off.'

In the past 22 years, Australian imports of goods and services from the US have exceeded our exports to that country by $260 billion. In the 18 years before the free-trade agreement came about, our trade deficit with the US averaged $10.95 billion a year; but in the four years since the USAFTA came into effect, our merchandise deficit with the US increased to $15.36 billion a year. I'd like to know when the first gains predicted by the CIE will kick in. We are starting from a long way behind zero after the first few years.

Mining the database to examine specific product groups shows that the USAFTA hasn't delivered the specific outcomes that were promised as part of what the Australian government of the day called 'this historic Agreement'.

Our exports of unprocessed and processed foods have already fallen during the agreement's short life — even though we were promised major improvements in access to the American market for our beef and agricultural products.

On top of this, we will certainly lose global sales as a consequence of the recent US decision to reintroduce subsidies on its dairy products. This event wasn't covered or considered in the agreement.

There have been a few Australian winners from the USAFTA. Officially, trade agreements aren't supposed to be about benefits for the few, but about an overall advantage for all sectors of the economies involved. Our industry policy for the past 30 years has been about creating economy-wide benefits, and the USAFTA was certainly promoted as achieving that intention.

The trade-deficit numbers quoted above are from our trade in physical merchandise. They do not include income payments and payments for intangibles such as royalties, management fees, technical service fees, and dividends. When those items are included, our deficit with the US is much worse. If the unreported obligations of US affiliates to their parent companies were also tallied, the total deficit of our trade with the United States would be frightening.

Our global balance-of-merchandise trade deficit in 2007–08 was only $17 billion, thanks to the minerals-exports bubble (which has probably already cost mining shareholders more than it gained). Our merchandise deficit with the US alone was almost $14 billion in that year, so we were almost square for physical goods, imports, and exports with the rest of the world for the first time in a very long time.

Analysis of merchandise trade doesn't take into account the potentially most devastating areas of one-way Australian market penetration created by the USAFTA.

The Australian Bureau of Statistic's economic indicator for 2007–08 shows that Australia's 'income' deficit in the balance of payments increased from $37 billion in 2005–06, to $45 billion in 2006–07, to $50 billion in 2007–08.

This is the statistical area where we simply don't know what is going on, except that we are paying out much more than we are receiving. If we are supposed to become a service economy, the income flow needs to be the other way; it certainly should not be rapidly deteriorating, as it is. The 2007–08 deficit was not far from 5 per cent of our national income.

The income areas include those where payments are often agreed by multinational affiliates. They also include the performing arts and the Pharmaceutical Benefits System, whereby the USAFTA requires consultation with the US before we introduce any measures that may inhibit US trade.

A NEO CLASSICAL ECONOMETRIC MODEL MUST ASSUME WHAT IT DOESN'T HAVE

A FREE TRADE ECONOMIST

Australian content in the performing arts was a major sticking point in the USAFTA negotiations. Australia, like many countries, has long had a system whereby media companies have been required to use a certain amount of local content. This prevented the media (particularly television) from simply buying masses of content from the US that was cheap, and well below the cost of production, because the producers had already sold it in their own country or in major markets such as the European Community.

This export of cultural content by the US or Europe is really the same as dumping coffee or sugar. The product exists, has already been sold into major markets, and can be marginally costed by the exporters as their fixed costs have already been recovered and can now be spread over additional sales. It doesn't matter how competitive you are — no industry can compete with dumped product. The World Trade Organisation bans dumping, but doesn't extend the concept to the performing arts.

The USAFTA outcome on the performing arts was that the US vets any change we want to make and can, apparently, effectively veto it. But we can't veto any restrictive measures that the Americans introduce.

The USAFTA also gave the United States the opportunity to directly engage in negotiations about inclusions of its pharmaceutical companies' drugs in our Pharmaceutical Benefits System.

The agreement has recently been used by the Australian government to prevent the introduction of a 'Buy Australian' campaign on the grounds that it breaches the USAFTA. We have changed a New South Wales government decision to give preference to Australian suppliers because of a US complaint.

But why does the US have the power to veto the New South Wales government decision, when we don't have the reciprocal power to veto the 'Buy American' policies that exist in almost every US state? The American negotiators managed to exclude US businesses with fewer than 1500 employees from the provisions of the USAFTA. In other words, they could continue to receive preference.

Why did Prime Minister Rudd tell us emphatically that we couldn't introduce a 'Buy Australian' campaign because it would result in retaliation? When has any country retaliated against an Australian trade policy? There have been dumping complaints, but that is not retaliation. That is a global process which involves hundreds of complaints a year about the breach of very specific rules agreed in the World Trade Organisation.

The Button Plans of the 1980s created quotas that decimated imports of cars and textiles, clothing, and footwear. No one retaliated. Australia is too good a market and too poor an exporter of value-added goods for countries to want to start a trade war with us. Once again, the cornerstone of Rudd government policy has been theoretical economics rather than evidence-based experience. Government rhetoric has collapsed when confronted by a small challenge from the United States.

If we are truly emerging from a fog of theory into some clean air of fact, we need to find out just what is going on in the PBS and the performing-arts trade under the USAFTA. We shouldn't treat the USAFTA as if it was cast in stone. It was created at another time with another government.

Times are tough in the crisis. We should know that. We don't need the millstone of the USAFTA-induced deficit around our neck to make them tougher. The US would walk away from the agreement in a heartbeat if it judged that it was in its sovereign interest to do so. We should adopt the same attitude.

We should at least ensure that labelling laws enable us to know where the products we buy have been grown or manufactured. It is tiresome to be constantly told in editorials that our manufacturing industry is a 'sheltered workshop' when we have annihilated assistance to it, and ignored the mechanisms that other countries use to protect their own workshops.

Solution #2: Do what the European Union and the US do, but do it better

Woolworths, Coles and, to a much smaller extent, IGA dominate the Australian food and grocery market. They state publicly that they have a preference for Australian produce and foodstuffs, but they drive a very hard bargain with their suppliers. Often, Australian producers are severely disadvantaged by the wage levels and working conditions that have been established for their rural workers, which are much higher than those in less-developed countries.

Woolworths and Coles charge their suppliers for space in their stores. This adversely affects small suppliers, who lack the capital to pay a levy for shelf space upfront — especially in circumstances where the retailer's orders may constitute more than half of their produce.

Trade unions, individuals, and various small organisations have tried a variety of 'Buy Australian' campaigns over the years. There is little doubt that most Australians prefer to buy Australian produce if the price is not much higher than that of imports; recently, it was claimed that as many as 85 per cent of Australians would do so in such circumstances.

Major retailers now show the origin of their vegetables, fruit, seafood, and nuts and, in some cases, use point-of-sale signs to explain why the entire product isn't sourced from Australia (as with, for example, prawns). The main issue is how to make sure consumers get the knowledge that helps them identify Australian products.

In 2009, the Minister for Trade, Simon Crean, received a study commissioned from the Centre for International Economics (CIE), which concluded that trade liberalisation over the past 20 years had benefited the average Australian family by $3900 a year. (This phoney precision is typical of free marketeers: for some reason, they never round up or down.)

This is the same consultancy that, in 2004, gave us the soon-to-be-rendered-nonsensical estimate of the multibillion-dollar gains per annum we would receive from the USAFTA. Crean's media and ALP conference headline-grabbing conclusion about the annual savings for an average family was based upon the CIE's view that 'it could be argued that manufacturing activity has actually increased as a result of reduced protection'. The basis for this is apparently the assumption that 'dynamic productivity and labour-market effects' have been realised. I have absolutely no idea what these dynamic effects are supposed to be. How can you measure them in dollar terms? How can we be certain that the impact has been passed through to the Australian family consumer?

Old free-market mumbo jumbo and the self-fulfilling modelling which results from limited assumptions are what we have been hearing for years, and now know so well.

Minister Crean has been annoyed by the decision of

both the European Union and the US to re-introduce dairy subsidies. We strongly objected in July 2009, but the US did it anyway. There has been no further flak since the fait accompli. We certainly didn't retaliate.

The USAFTA imposed less-than-strenuous conditions for the removal of US tariffs on beef and dairy produce: the time-period for their gradual reduction to zero was 18 years. Of course, a subsidy is likely to more than completely negate any tariff reduction over such a long period.

The two major Australian producers of dairy produce are Murray Goulburn, an Australian co-operative of dairy farmers, and a New Zealand-owned company, Fonterra. Murray Goulburn earns half its revenue from exports. And yet European and US subsidies impact directly on exports, as suppliers compete against each other in online auctions. Prices fell by 16 per cent in the first weeks of June 2009, against a backdrop of overseas subsidies that are likely to be worth over $1000 a tonne for milk powder.

Simon Crean has said that this action flies in the face of the commitment of G20 leaders not to impose protectionist measures and that, not to worry, concluding the Doha Round of multilateral-trade negotiations will fix the export-subsidies problem by eliminating them completely.

Sugar quotas and agricultural subsidies, which were assumed to be part of the USAFTA by the CIE model (sugar wasn't included in the agreement), are supposed to be eliminated when Doha finally gets up. That will be in the year 2050, when whatever the successor body is called will probably turn the same blind eye on major nation international-trading practices that the WTO does.

How can anyone say that manufacturing in Australia has

expanded in the past 20 years? Nevertheless, the mouse that roared has expressed Australia's objections at the relevant embassies. Tony Burke, the Minister for Agriculture, Fisheries and Forestry, saw things more clearly, saying: 'This is another kick in the guts for our dairy farmers, following the recent EU decision as well.'

Having a 'Buy Australian' campaign is not really up there with agricultural subsidies, but minister Crean used CIE's modelling of a banner-number savings-figure of about $4000 to oppose it. Once again, we need to look at the assumptions in the model. In February 2009, CIE published a study on 'Climate Policy in the years to come, in the context of the century to follow'. I suppose that if they can model that, it is a breeze to conclude that manufacturing has grown in the past 20 years and that everybody is better off to the tune of exactly $3900.

Agricultural subsidies (the Common Agricultural Policy in Europe, and the farm-subsidies legislation in America) have been in operation in Europe and the US since before World War II. These subsidies have represented as much as half of the total revenue received by their farmers; not surprisingly, attempts to remove the subsidies have been the major stumbling blocks in earlier rounds of trade negotiations, which have been stalled since the 1960s.

Japan and Korea also have very substantial non-tariff barriers that prevent the import of agricultural products. These barriers are not made public, but are very effective. For example, when Australia wanted to export rice to Japan some years ago, the Japanese government demurred, but Australia persisted. The result was that the Japanese government purchased about $40 million of Australian rice, and then warehoused it for a few years. Eventually, they trialled it in a small way. Strangely enough, consumers didn't like the stale rice, and the official view was expressed that there was no Japanese-consumer acceptance of our rice.

Any study of world trade-flows between countries will demonstrate that there are domestic markets that are simply reserved for local producers. You still don't see Italian Fiats in France, or Japanese cars in Korea. Even though the tariffs are low, imported cars are virtually non-existent. Similarly, an Asahi beer in Korea is much more expensive than an Oriental Breweries' beer.

If we can't beat the rest of the world, we should join it on agricultural subsidies. The most efficient and controllable way of doing this is literally in the aisles of the major chain stores. If the major retailers are given a subsidy, they will buy Australian produce. The task is then to ensure that they give the farmer a price that reflects the subsidy. Giving the subsidy to the retailers rather than the farmers is much more administratively efficient. We already do this when we tax our two major breweries, rather than hotels, clubs, and liquor stores. We produce the greenest, cleanest, least diseased, and least pest-ridden food in the world. Surely we can put it in a can, a packet, or a jar, and sell it to our own population.

We also have no knowledge of overseas practices for the sale of assets and property (particularly large tracts of arable land), and should learn from and follow the lead of the US, the EU, Japan, and Korea, particularly when owners are either placed in administration or bankrupted.

Our bankruptcies are fire sales that liquidate company assets at very low prices. By contrast, bankruptcies in the US take two forms: Chapter 11 bankruptcies, which are about rehabilitating the bankrupt company so that it can trade again; and Chapter 7 bankruptcies, which involve the irrecoverable liquidation of assets.

The courts are much more involved in the US process than they are in Australia. The receivers in Australia have had carte blanche to do as they wish for a long time. For example, in the 1991 recession, the Australian banks used first-tier accountancy firms as the receivers. The banks got so little return from the process (after paying the receivers' fees) that the next time the market was in difficulty, they quarantined debts and tried to trade out some of their customers' financial problems. In 1995, 25 per cent of New South Wales hotels were in administration, but the introduction of poker machines and the subsequent revenue from this source fixed their problems.

Companies under administration usually have their owners and managers operating the business, and the administrators try to return the business to the owners as a viable operation. Receivers, however, protect the interests of the creditors. Few companies come out of receivership. Liquidation is the final stage, at which point assets are sold and distributed to pay the costs of the liquidators, receivers, and administrators. Whatever is left is paid to the creditors—beginning with employee entitlements, then tax obligations, then secured creditors, and finally unsecured creditors.

The obvious problem is that the liquidators' goals are not the goals of the Australian economy. Their first aim is to collect their own fees. Their second aim is to collect enough money to pay outstanding employee entitlements. Their third aim is to pay the company's statutory obligations, such as GST and company tax. They then pay secured creditors, and then unsecured creditors get what's left (which is usually nothing). The liquidators have no social or national goals. They sell to whoever will pay the most and the fastest, regardless of their location or nationality. They act in the national interest only if the government forces them to.

I was at Deloitte in 1990 when they were the Fairfax receivers. Des Nicholls, the managing partner of the insolvency group, told me that both secured and unsecured creditors had received a hundred cents in the dollar. My reply was that this only proved they should never have been placed in receivership by their banks in the first place. Conrad Black, the Canadian entrepreneur presently serving a jail sentence, made over $300 million out of the fire sale of the Fairfax assets.

Solution #3: Add value to our mineral exports

In 1975, a consortium of BHP, Bethlehem Steel, British Steel, Nippon Steel, and Kaiser Steel spent $2 million on a feasibility study to develop a major semi-manufactures plant at White River in Western Australia. Their idea was to use Australian iron ore and coking coal to produce blooms, billets, and slabs of steel for sale in export markets. Before they proceeded to spend $40 million on a detailed study, they asked the federal government if it would contribute by building the necessary rail infrastructure to the local port. The plant would have employed 40,000 people.

The Fraser government refused to contemplate such an investment; instead, the plant was located in Brazil, by an entity known as the Gerdau Group. Gerdau now manufactures more than 25 million metric tonnes of steel in its plants in Brazil, Paraguay, and North America. It has more than 30,000 employees and 10,000 service-providers.

The export income from the stillborn White River Plant would have been of the order of $10 billion a year (at present-day values) over the past 30 years. This single piece of infrastructure would have more than halved our foreign debt and massively reduced our exposure to the GFD.

'What ifs' don't mean much, except when they define the character of an economy or a succession of governments. In 1975, we were at the beginning of the no-government-intervention obsession (other than for political purposes, of course).

Since then, we have been digging the ore up and shipping it out. The financiers love digging up and shipping mineral ores. Adding value to the ore carries a risk, whereas they would rather confine their risks to selling short and trading in derivatives. Low freight-to-value ratios mean that the value of the ore shipped is about equal to the cost of the shipping, compliance, and other logistics services needed to get the product from the mine to the overseas mill. This means that the shipping companies (who earn most of their income offshore, have their ships built offshore, and use foreign crews), the railways, and the road-transport companies all make as much as the miners for dealing in bulk ores and coal. The price of the freight from the Pilbara to China is as much as the price for the iron ore.

In the 2009 budget, the Rudd government matched the contribution of the Western Australian government to build a rail line from the site of major iron-ore resources to the export port at Oakajee. This is all very well, but there has been no suggestion that we should attempt to add value to these or any other mineral exports. BHP Billiton and Fortescue are content to let the Chinese mills add value.

And yet, only by adding value (which is essentially by applying further labour inputs) will we be able to overcome the tyranny of distance and its associated costs, which make us uncompetitive with other sources of supply.

The present 'export the raw materials' approach is a blind policy driven by self-interested and multinational–led interest groups such as the Australian Mining Industry Council, which has watched the massive growth in overseas-owned iron and steel industries whilst stunting the growth of our own value-added industries.

In 2001, the ABS published its last general review of foreign ownership in Australia. It calculated that 42 per cent of the Australian mining industry was owned by US companies. I wonder what the percentage is in 2010.

Conclusion

A feature of both world wars during the previous century was that the populations of the nations in conflict were told that the conflicts would be over and won within months. Instead, they lasted for five years and six years respectively, and not everybody won. Negative attitudes amongst the populations were, at worse, regarded as traitorous and, at best, frowned upon.

The Great Depression started in 1930 and ended at the beginning of World War II. If this really is the worst economic downturn since then, why are most commentators saying that it is already over?

In our combined *Brave New World/1984*, we are all victims of the Ministry of Truth and a compliant media, but at least we have the soma of alcohol, television, and football to keep us unquestioning and passive while the rulers go about their business.

The great unknown remains how much of the sub-prime iceberg lies below the surface of the world economies. It is unlikely that the most scandalous sub-prime loans—those made to people who had absolutely no hope of meeting the payments—have emerged and been met by huge government interventions to prop up the Fannie Maes and Freddie Macs that simply couldn't be allowed to fail.

In 1997, the Australian Business Foundation published a study it had commissioned into Australia's future, titled 'The High Road or the Low Road'. The study concluded that Australia's better path to growth was to focus on high-tech production. It was preceded by another study by Pappas, Carter, Evans and Koop in the late 1980s, called 'The Global Challenge: Australian Manufacturing in the Nineties', which concluded that Australia didn't export enough elaborately transformed manufactures.

The federal government is following a familiar path with its commitment to university research and development, and the creation of co-operative research centres, focusing on 'world-class collaborative research and innovation'. Part of its plan is to make scholarships available for 1000 students, regardless of where they come from.

Studies by academics and consultants have an inherent bias towards clean and clever industries. The problem is that not all Australians are clean and clever. We do, however, have a country that is rich in resources. We also have a very high standard of living, and are isolated from each other's state markets and world markets in general.

It seems stupid to decide that we will ship low-value, high-freight-cost raw materials to the rest of the world, and think about outgunning the Japanese, Americans, Europeans, and Koreans in high-tech products. The first industry that the Tariff Board killed in its 1972 general review of manufacturing was electronics. At the time, only Japan, the US, and Holland had the global market-share and subsequent ability to finance research and development into electronic components and new products. The same situation applies today in the case of pharmaceuticals and most global brands of consumer products. We lack the domestic market-size to justify the local manufacture of such items.

When you think about it, our strength lies in our resources and agricultural products. It seems obvious that we should add value to those products, and try to export them. We have been successful with wine, but we haven't tried to do much else. Believe it or not, wine is now counted as an elaborately transformed manufacture, and makes such export figures look better than they really are.

The Australian market for processed food and beverages is currently dominated by global manufacturers that have bought local manufacturers and brand names. In some cases, they have gradually run down local manufacture and have eventually closed the Australian entity. It is fascinating to watch the slow process of attrition and withdrawal that they go through. They are in no hurry to leave, but they do leave in the end. Their strategy is all about winding down the workforce, and watching the best and brightest workers leave in the meantime. These are the ones who will be most troublesome when the time comes to negotiate closure.

Sometimes the multinational investor waits a few years to develop tax losses that then create a tax holiday when they return with a vengeance with the imported product made from Australian raw materials and bearing the Australian brand name. This is one of the beauties of transfer pricing. The multinationals have a level of flexibility with pricing that is simply not available to an Australian-owned company.

This may sound jaundiced; but, after 30 years of working for multinationals and being involved in ATO audits and settlements for the past ten years, I have to be jaundiced. Most of us don't understand the financial capacity of a global company to stonewall its way through a difficult situation until the years of audit are long past and the original team has moved on.

Most of my legal battles on behalf of multinationals with Customs or the ATO lasted between four and seven years each. My clients had the money to pay for the Queen's Counsels and Senior Counsels. They had enough money at stake to run the gauntlet of the legal process, starting with a brief to counsel, then through the Administrative Appeals Tribunal, to the Federal Court, to the full bench of the Federal Court, to seeking leave to appeal to the High Court, to the High Court itself. They didn't pay interest as a matter of course. Receiving interest involved another legal battle. Taxing legal costs (that is, determining how much of the winning side's legal costs would be borne by the loser) was a further battle.

Australian companies are generally small-to-medium-sized businesses. They can't afford the management time or the money to run this process to the bitter end. Perhaps one thing we should do is reduce the levels of appeal that are available, or limit the types of legal matters that are allowed go forward on appeal.

Australia's mass production of manufactures should be in materials made of steel, copper, and aluminium, and in rural produce. We do, however, need to do a much better job of selling our products to Asia. We have tended to do things our way rather than their way.

Australians should own the companies that produce such things. The Americans, English, French, Germans, Japanese, Koreans, Chinese, and Indians haven't sold their successful companies and assets to each other. We, on the other hand, have been selling successful Australian companies to overseas investors for a long time, and are now into the third decade of selling our infrastructure overseas.

Probably the greatest lesson that history teaches us is that power elites decay and decline. Economist Joseph Schumpeter's concept of 'creative destruction' advanced the idea that a new economy was built on the ruins of the old. His theory is the foundation of the free-market economists' core belief that we should simply walk away from the carnage of the global financial disaster and, hand in hand with the short sellers and those who sold their businesses at inflated prices and now have cash, create a new economy. These winners will be the next power elite.

The past 35 years have been a time of major micro-economic reform and deregulation in Australia, and in the industrial economies of the world. But that job is done, and what was genuinely valuable in economic reform has been achieved. Such an achievement, as always, has come at a cost to the structure and nature of our nation. We are not as egalitarian as we were before, and we often confuse media spin or an incomprehensible economic model with the truth.

We are now living in a post-disaster interregnum, when apologists are denying that the global financial disaster was the fault of the financial-sector elite and the economists. Many of them are in powerful places, and still hold sway over governments.

The empirical evidence is that the reformers of past decades have now become the establishment. Their power elite has had a major shock, but they are trying to do what elites have always tried to do: defend their power base, and continue to rule.

I have always loved the speech in the movie *Blade Runner* when the fabulous replicant Roy says, 'Time to die.' He has seen everything and done everything, and his body clock has stopped.

We have seen the economic and social change that has been wrought by the free-market economists. Some of it was good. Some of it was bad. They, of course, thought that it was all good. They also think that their reforms are not finished and that their power model is intact. This is not true.

Every historical theory and elite has, up until now, had a use-by date, after which the theory delivers only trivial new benefits, and the elite degenerates. Free-market economics is no different from what has gone before.

The most productive changes introduced by free-market economics have now been in place for more than ten years. The real economies of Australia and the rest of the world are volatile, and this makes economic modelling and accurate projections impossible. Some of the major arguments for governments not to intervene in markets have been exposed as nonsense. This applies particularly to the concepts that all consumers are rational, and that the privatisation of state assets and infrastructure was a major step forward in micro-economic reform and deregulation. The merchant banks kept the rewards, and left governments with the risks.

The global financial disaster has been an icy-cold shower for the world. Those who used to say (and still proclaim) that the government should do nothing in the private sector have asked for more help and more intervention by government than any other group has ever sought. Ironically, they have become the greatest rent-seekers of them all. They have also turned back the clock and negotiated their assistance from government behind closed doors. There has been no Productivity Commission inquiry into assistance for the Australian financial sector. We won't get a report on the dealings of the Treasury, the Future Fund, and the Reserve Bank with the four major banks. The review of the chaos of our superannuation funds won't involve public hearings.

These government interventions have all been and will be cosy deals, in back rooms where the only difference between now and 1920 (the year before the Tariff Board began operations) is the absence of smoke.

It's time for the economist technocrats to get back to research and reality. We need evidence-based policy, and we need to test theories empirically. Economics must take the next step and become a practical science.

KEVIN RUDD'S BEST SHIRT
(A FREE TRADERS GUIDE)

1. WHAT DID HE PAY FOR IT? $99·00

2. HOW MUCH DID THE RETAILER GET? $45·00

3. HOW MUCH DID THE IMPORTER GET? $17-80

4. HOW MUCH DID THE E.U. OWNER OF THE BRAND GET? $25·00

5. HOW MUCH DID THE CHINESE MANUFACTURER GET? $1-50

PLUS A LITTLE FOR THE CHINESE WORKER: 50¢

6. HOW MUCH TARIFF PROTECTION DID THOSE SHIFTY "RENT SEEKING" AUSTRALIAN TEXTILE MANUFACTURERS GET? 20¢

i.e. 10% ON CUSTOMS VALUE OF THE SHIRT - $2·00

SPOONER

A User's Guide to Picking Losers the Free-Market Economics Way

One of the commandments of free-market economics is: governments shall not attempt to pick winners in the economy, as they are always wrong. A second commandment seems to be: only neo-liberals, their think-tanks, and like-minded government instrumentalities shall pick winners, because they know best and can predict the future.

This appendix provides an Australian users' guide to the *Feilopaedia of Losers Picked by Free-Market Economists Over the Past 30 Years*. The grand prize goes to the Global Financial Disaster of 2007–09.

The GFD was a direct result of the dominance of free-market economics in government policy. Consequently, government failed to intervene and stop the biggest financial scam in the history of the world and its spread to all the industrialised countries through collateralised debt obligations packages that are, fundamentally, worth nothing or very little.

The tariff review (1970)

The Tariff Board had been a sleepy hollow for 50 years before its chairman, Alf Rattigan, discovered a way to wake it up. Instead of waiting for the government to ask it to inquire into an industry, the board convinced the government that it should review all manufacturing industry against a common standard called 'effective rates of assistance'. This stratagem transformed the Tariff Board into the Industries Assistance Commission, doubled its staff, and gave it work for the next 20 years. It also gave the commission certainty because it knew what the outcome of its reviews would be before they started: tariffs would be lowered. No industry ever got a higher level of assistance out of the tariff-review programme.

Effective rates of assistance

This was a very clever and complex idea. The only problem was that it didn't work. It was based on the fact that duty rates in the Customs tariff simply increased the landed cost of imports generally by a percentage amount (*ad valorem* rates). Instead, according to the commission, real assistance to Australian industry had to be focused on the Australian value-added component in the manufacturing process. For example, timber merchants used to resaw large flitches of Douglas Fir to create smaller timber pieces for the building industry. If the imported timber cost, say, $45, the local resawing costs would have been an extra $5. Providing protection through the 40 per cent tariff rate gave the merchants an effective rate of 360 per cent ($18 of duty to protect $5 of local value added).

The effective-rate concept was connected to two other

ideas. The first was that the government should not intervene in the economy in the allocation of scarce resources of land, labour, and capital. (Neutral resource-allocation theory is discussed below.) The second idea was that if industries which couldn't compete without excessive government assistance were phased out, the resources thereby released would flow to much more competitive industries.

The problem was that the resource-flow didn't happen. We never created the internationally competitive, outward-looking manufacturing industries that the manufacturing review was set up to create.

The tariff-review programme sorted industries by effective rates into high-, medium-, and low-assistance industries. The highly assisted industries were reviewed first. The preconception was that, if they needed the high rate, they had to be inefficient.

Neutral resource-allocation theory

The next new idea within the Industries Assistance Commission was that government intervention via assistance to industry should be neutral across all manufacturing industry. This meant that the government had to intervene through the manufacturing-industry review once and for all to create a level playing field for all manufacturers. At that stage, the commission hadn't dreamt about reforming the financial sector, the services sector, or the professions. It still hasn't.

The commission believed that, if industries' nominal tariffs resulted in high effective rates, the lowering of those rates would see the industries contract or close, because they were inefficient. This would release their resources of land, labour, and capital, and the freed resources would be captured by the industries that were most efficient.

ORANI and other models

Since 1975, the federal government has spent more than $20 million at Monash University and other institutions in a bid to have them model the input-output impact that closing inefficient industries would have on Australia's gross national product.

This process occurred just as economics faculties at the major Australian universities started introducing econometrics as a compulsory subject in an economics degree. For numerate rather than literate students, it was the way to honours and higher degrees. Professor Alan Powell at Monash showed that, with the creation of the ORANI model, modelling could be a lucrative profession which did not have to relate to the real world as long as certain assumptions were rigorously followed.

For the next 20 years, the Industry Commission used economic modelling to forecast the consumer-price impact of tariff reductions. The results were always positive, because the model assumed that released resources would flow to the most profitable and efficient economic activities in Australia. The modellers never assumed that the displaced resources might lie idle for a decade or two, or even flow to some less productive activity. No assumptions were made about the removal of commercial value from human beings' discarded or displaced skill-sets, and the failure of displaced workers to find another job immediately.

Consequently, the forecasts were never correct; instead, the gains were, generally, totally appropriated in the supply chain. Only when the reduction was very substantial did some portion of the foregone duty trickle down to the consumer.

Gough Whitlam's 25 per cent tariff cut

Prime minister Gough Whitlam declared he was 'a Rattigan man', and weighed in with a unilateral tariff cut of 25 per cent. There was no justification for the extent of the reduction, and no legislation to force importers and retailers to pass on the cost-reduction to Australian consumers. This was a major opportunity missed to create a precedent to ensure that tariff reductions benefited Australian consumers, rather than the overseas suppliers and the local distributors of the goods.

By the time the Whitlam government left office, there was no stopping the Tariff Board. With its new moniker as the Industries Assistance Commission, its staff had doubled, and about a hundred inquiries were partially completed. The review programme had an unstoppable impetus.

Free trade

Free-trade rhetoric has been a standard tool of neo-liberal propaganda for the past 40 years. But there never has been free trade, and there never will be until the world becomes one country under one government with one currency and one set of laws.

The reason that the expression 'free trade' has been so frequently and inaccurately used is that it has a powerful emotional impact on the listener or reader. It sounds highly desirable.

Anyone who practises in the area of international trade

knows that tariffs have been reducing since 1970. They also know that tariffs have been replaced by a number of non-tariff barriers, which have increased in both number and impact. Studies in the European Union show that as tariffs fell, they were replaced by non-tariff measures that have proved an even more significant barrier to imports.

These measures include the imposition of national standards, which require international manufacturers to interrupt their production-runs to satisfy the requirements of individual markets, and thereby limit the economies of scale available when production is carried out on a global basis.

Other cost-adding measures include taxes to restrain emissions; individual marking and commerce-description rules for packaging; notification rules for the arrival of containers; and the requirement that importers provide full details of the chain of supply, and the names and addresses of the workers involved, virtually back to the farm or factory.

'Voluntary quantitative restrictions' are also used, which is fancy language for quotas that aren't really voluntary. If the exporter doesn't agree to restrict exports to an aggrieved country, the explicit threat becomes more direct, and stringent restrictions are applied. This was the case when China banned the import of Japanese motor vehicles in the late 1990s. The Chinese importers praised the action of the state, as they were going bankrupt.

Simply slowing down the supply chain through technical Customs queries, making demands for additional information, and routinely engaging in the dilatory clearance of goods by the authorities is another common non-tariff weapon. In the case of perishable products, this may result in the loss of the entire shipment.

Border security has been the engine of growth for Customs and other port authorities since 11 September 2001. The growth of security-related government bureaucracies is the most potent non-tariff barrier to international trade. In reality, trade liberalisation has been off the agenda since 2001.

Free-trade agreements

The only trade compact that Australia has which comes close to a genuine free-trade agreement is the Closer Economic Relations (CER) agreement we have with New Zealand. CER replaced the New Zealand–Australia Free Trade Agreement (NAFTA), which began in the 1960s. Of course, there were exemptions from the NAFTA, but only in relation to products that were the most important—such as New Zealand *Pinus radiata* timber.

The CER has led to all merchandise trade between the two countries being free of duty, so long as it can be established that the 'rules of origin' have been satisfied.

These rules apply to all our 'free-trade agreements'. Basically, there has to be substantial transformation of the goods in the country of origin, where more than 50 per cent of the factory or works costs has to occur; and, in some cases, there must be direct shipment from the country of origin. This is certainly the case in the USAFTA, where the direct-shipment rule has been used to transfer rum-bottling operations from Europe, for example, to Puerto Rico.

Of course, the CER doesn't have any influence whatsoever on the trade in services, or on barriers preventing the two-way flow of doctors, lawyers, accountants, and other professionals between Australia and New Zealand.

213

Australia's other free-trade agreements are with Thailand, Singapore, Chile, the ASEAN countries, and the United States. The Minister for Trade, Simon Crean, is also negotiating such agreements with China, the Gulf countries, Japan, South Korea, and Malaysia. Also under consideration are agreements with India and Indonesia. Given the level of government intervention in these economies, 'free' is hardly an appropriate word for the likely outcomes. Our agreement with Thailand has already created substantial friction amongst Australian manufacturers, who have found that 'free' means 'unfree', and that some two-way trade is really only one-way.

The Productivity Commission has said that these free-trade agreements should just be called trade agreements. The commission would undoubtedly be frustrated by the barriers (including some tariffs) that remain between Australia and the countries listed above, especially in the much-vaunted USAFTA. The agreements have turned out to be not much good at overcoming non-tariff barriers in both merchandise and services trade. Mr Crean might be happy that the tariff barriers are coming down, but the only trade-agreement partner that the agreements mean a lot to is Australia.

Simon Crean is a Labor politician of considerable integrity who is committed to the objectives of his portfolio. He does not countenance any reservations about them. That's a shame, because to negotiate the free-trade-agreement world while protecting the national interest requires the subtlety of a Machiavelli and the diplomacy of a Talleyrand. The minister doesn't combine those qualities—otherwise he might have become the prime minister when Labor's latest drover's dog won government.

Measuring the 'benefits' of a free-trade agreement is

relatively easy in the case of merchandise trade: just wait a few years, and then look at the trend in imports and exports. The USAFTA data is a perfect case-study.

Multilateral trade agreements

There has been a significant shift in Australia's approach to trade agreements over the past ten years. Before then, it was regarded as ideologically wrong to enter into bilateral agreements, rather than multilateral agreements. This has changed since the USAFTA: we now have agreements, as we've seen, with several countries, pending agreements with others, and a multilateral agreement with the ASEAN countries. The minister for trade has been very busy.

My view is that these countries have worked out that we are very earnest about our trade agreements, and they have seen how the US, Singapore, and Thailand have been able to ramp up their trade and investment in Australia since the agreements started. There seems to be an almost indecent scramble to sign up with Australia. The existing agreements have resulted in an increase of about $10 billion a year in our current-account deficit.

In practice, the trade agreements are of limited value. Only a few years ago, Indonesia resorted to using a Swiss company to examine shipments to Indonesia prior to their export from the country of origin. The cross-border duty process for importers has always been subject to the 'interpretations' of individual Indonesian Customs officers. Anecdotal evidence suggests a similar experience is being incurred with Thailand.

Unilateral trade liberalisation

This concept was pushed in the 1990s by two former chairmen of what is now the Productivity Commission—Alf Rattigan, architect of the manufacturing-industry review started by the Tariff Board, and his then-chief of staff, Bill Carmichael, who went on to become chair of the Industry Commission. They condemned the 'backsliders'—countries that had been tardy with tariff reforms—and suggested that Australia should simply drop its barriers to them, regardless.

Their argument was that this action would result in the rapid creation of a new, more competitive Australian economy. It would have, too; the only problem was that the new economy would have been much smaller than the economy it replaced, and a lot of people would have been unemployed. Of course, 'creative destruction' is part of the hymn book of neo-liberalism. No doubt, operators of the calibre of Rattigan and Carmichael would have lived well in the new economy, but what about the rest of us? Luckily, successive Australian governments weren't persuaded to follow this advice.

One of the great assets of free-market economics is its myopia. The conventional free-market wisdom is that those who are poorly educated or trained, or who live in the wrong place, should simply get educated, move, and change jobs. But life doesn't work that way for most of us.

Unilateral trade liberalisation would undoubtedly increase global income, but there are obvious winners and losers. I would like to see the political leaders of the US, Japan, and the EU tell their farmers that they planned to unilaterally eliminate import barriers to their goods, and eliminate subsidies to them. It would be a very good way to lose government very fast.

Economic rationalism

This concept was the early version of free-market economics or neo-liberalism. The Industries Assistance Commission had considerable difficulty in explaining to witnesses at public hearings the difference between nominal tariffs (the rates in the third schedule of the Customs Tariff Act, also called 'the working tariff') and the concept of effective rates, with its focus on the actual percentage rate of assistance accorded to local manufacture.

To some extent, this friction created a siege mentality within the commission, and its adoption of the presumption that the commission's conclusion was rational and that the industry view was not. The commission attempted to explain effective rates and the concept of neutral resource-allocation in annual reports and various papers.

The commission ultimately realised that no benchmark tariff, regardless of how low it might be (other than zero) would provide a neutral level of assistance to all industries. Those industries with high local value-added characteristics would always receive less effective assistance than those industries that assembled their products from imported components. This would effectively distort the allocation of resources in the market to industries that were the least efficient.

Economist and early free-trade guru Professor Max Corden had originally suggested benchmark tariff-levels as a means of moving towards tariff neutrality. In its early days, the commission followed this concept with a 'tops-down' theory to move first to a tariff benchmark of 25 per cent and then to a benchmark of 15 per cent. This meant that all tariffs above 25 per cent would be phased down to the lower level.

The commission talked about but never applied a 'bottoms-up' theory (that is, that all tariffs below 25 per cent would be phased up to that level). Apart from destroying the effective-rate theory, this would have resulted in the essential nonsense of applying duty rates to goods that were not manufactured in Australia, and therefore were already entering the country under by-laws (subsequently called tariff concessions), either free of duty or subject to what was then regarded as a negligible rate (3 per cent).

The rationalist concept was founded on the idea that industries should receive a common level of assistance against imports, as different assistance-rates gave one industry a government-induced advantage over another in the market struggle to attract resources of land, labour, and capital. The concept was, of course, impossible to apply in practice through the manufacturing-industry review programme: industries waiting in the queue for review were advantaged by the simple fact that their turn for a tariff reduction had not arrived.

Essentially, 'rationalism' was another fine word (like 'free' and 'liberal') that was applied to philosophies which weren't rational at all. The rational approach to resource allocation in terms of market efficiency was a rate of zero, and the elimination of any government intervention or regulation. As it happens, it is precisely this scorched-earth policy, and its pursuit by free-market zealots (regardless of the limitations of the theory's assumptions in the market place), which has led to Australia's exposure to the global financial disaster. It has also been the commission's approach since the mid-1990s: obdurate as ever, it still regards any request for assistance as 'rent-seeking'.

Decades of unremitting tariff-lowering — without the erection or retention of compensating non-tariff barriers—have led to entirely predictable adverse results. Imports have increased their share of virtually every market within Australia for merchandise goods. This has resulted in negative current-account balances for every year since 1973. In turn, these negative balances have created a known foreign debt of $700 billion, and further unknown debt-amounts in the accounts of banks and subsidiaries of multinational firms. And now overseas banking failures are being directly transmitted to Australia as the lenders fail, or curtail their lending.

The Cairns Group, the Kennedy Round, and the Doha Round

Global free trade has been the dream of every naive and ignorant academic economist for the past 50 years. It has an air of slightly more reality than Esperanto—the dream of a global language.

Since president Kennedy launched the Kennedy Round of international trade negotiations in 1962, there has been a continuous, expensive programme of learned papers, programmes, and meetings all over the world to pursue the chimera of free trade. The basic obstacle has been the division between the developing countries and the developed countries over the treatment of agricultural products.

The Doha Round of trade negotiations started in 2001. Australia is a leading member of the Cairns Group of negotiators, which consists of most of South America, Canada, Thailand, Indonesia, Malaysia, and the Philippines. The group has been lobbying for free-market access for agricultural products, and the end of subsidies in the European Union and the US, for the past 40 years. Both rounds have foundered on this issue, although hope still springs eternal for its resolution in the Doha Round. Meanwhile, in May 2009, the EU and the US both reintroduced dairy-product subsidies, and they have never discontinued their sugar subsidies.

The developed countries are content with the present situation. They get to keep protecting their farmers while lobbying for lower tariff and non-tariff barriers in developing countries. Australia is one out, because it has dismantled its quantitative restrictions on sugar, and has deregulated its dairy industry. We are highly regarded by the other developed countries for doing this, and they keep saying that they will think about following our example.

Selling government assets

Deregulation and micro-economic reform were the battle cries of free-market economists in the 1980s and 1990s. Tariff reductions, the sale of state assets and businesses, and the withdrawal of government from the market place were seen as the only way to improve the efficiency and productivity of the Australian economy.

There is no doubt that Australia had to move forward from the post-World War II environment in which trade unionism, high tariffs, subsidies, quotas, temporary assistance, jobs for life, six o'clock closing, and no work for married women were the order of the day.

There is equally no doubt that, sooner or later, the reform process became self-defeating. While the industrialised countries of the world introduced non-tariff measures, impeded excessive foreign ownership, and stopped short of eliminating major agricultural subsidies, Australia went ahead and stopped the lot. We are really a guileless country. The Productivity Commission and Treasury are like the legendary salt mill that never stopped grinding, and eventually made the seas salty. The commitment to 'reform' by the elitist group in these places has never faltered. Of course, if it did, they would be out of a job.

The present Labor government has continued with what is now a very tired, outdated approach to growing the Australian economy. Its watchwords are 'innovation' and 'productivity improvement'. These weapons are particularly suited to fostering growth in manufacturing industries, but the Australian economy has moved a long way from its former emphasis on manufacturing.

The problems I have with the deification of innovation and productivity are dealt with elsewhere in this book. The basic fact is that we have done most of what needed to be done in this area, and there is now very little gain and a substantial social cost involved in taking this approach any further.

Training and labour mobility

The present policy-view is that we need to create a labour force that is constantly being retrained, and that is very adaptable and very mobile. This sounds great, but what about the lifestyle? It would be interesting to survey the senior staff of Treasury and the Productivity Commission to find out how many different jobs they have had, and how many times they have worked away from Canberra, Sydney, or Melbourne.

The awkward fact is that training and labour mobility create significant social costs for families. Very few people are willing to have their business and personal lives in a state of constant flux or change, if they have a choice about it: their children want to attend the same schools; the families want to keep their circle of friends; and the parents have obligations and blood-ties to their own parents and grandchildren.

Why would anyone think that the labour force in general would agree to the idea? Most people regard work as a necessary interruption to their lives. They don't propose to spend their free time being trained for an occupation they find mundane or boring, or constantly packing up, taking the kids out of school, and moving to a location where there is new work—just because the government tells them it's in the economy's interest that they do so.

Bringing in guest workers (and sending call centres offshore)

A major study titled 'Australia's Demographic Challenges', published by the federal Treasury in 2004, clearly demonstrated that our population is ageing and that our birth rate is falling.

In 1968, the average life-expectancy of an Australian man was 68. In 1997, it was 78. In 2042, it is expected to be 83. Women live, on average, seven years longer than men.

In 1972, the Australian fertility rate was 2.7 births per woman. In 1997, it had fallen to 1.7 births per thousand. This is substantially below the traditional Malthusian calculation that the rate has to be two per thousand every year if population levels are to remain static.

We are living longer, and producing fewer children. This change is a feature of all industrialised economies. By 2042, Treasury predicts that our population over 65 will double and that our traditional workforce aged between 15 and 64 won't increase at all.

The consequences of this population trend were identified by Treasury, with its usual heroic predictions of their impact on the budget. Without migration, our population will fall. Health and aged-care spending will double. According to Treasury, the pharmaceutical benefits subsidy will increase from half a per cent of GDP in 2004 (at a cost of $4.5 billion per annum) to 3.5 per cent in 2042 ($70 billion). We will have a budget deficit of $40 billion instead of a surplus of $10 billion.

The budgetary options presented by Treasury were to increase personal income-tax collections by 40 per cent, eliminate the entire health budget, or create more debt and a much larger current-account deficit.

One solution for those who are 55 or older who don't have sufficient superannuation is to forget about retirement. In 2009, the qualifying age for the aged pension was increased to 67, although this will not be introduced immediately. The alternative (or perhaps a parallel solution) is to increase migration, or to allow the temporary residence of foreign workers and their families.

The latter solution is a good example of us coming up with the wrong answer to the right question.

This is an emotional issue, and in discussing it we need to steer very clear of national and religious stereotypes. We must, as the old saying goes, 'populate or perish'. But we should not import New Kanakas or a Pacific version of the United States' Mexicans. And we should not send jobs offshore that can be performed in Australia with a higher quality of customer service.

Encouraging migration and using the temporary services of foreign workers are the embodiments of two very different philosophies. In the former, there is a commitment both by the migrants and the community they are entering that they will start a new life in a new country and become Australians. Both sides know that there will always be assimilation problems, but the intention is to create a permanent relationship. There is no going back.

Foreign workers do not come on this basis. They may bring their families with them, but the plan is to deploy them in a particular occupation and, ultimately, to send them back to their foreign homes. The fundamental argument of policy-makers in this area is that migrant workers possess skills and occupational experience that are inadequately supplied by the Australian workforce. They are not supposed to replace Australians in the workforce on a permanent basis.

The foreign-workforce issue should not be confused with the conflict that regularly occurs over decisions to relocate local business activities in overseas call centres. That is another manifestation of our demographic dilemma, which needs separate analysis.

From the late 1940s, we have embraced migration. We began with displaced Europeans after the war, and have changed over time to welcome Eastern Europeans, Asians, and Africans. They have enriched our society and expanded our economy.

But the jury is out on foreign workers.

There are already some hundreds of thousands of students and temporary visitors in Australia who are either working for low wages or providing income for empty-nesters with spare rooms.

One problem is that the Department of Immigration seems to be a good gatekeeper, but is not so good at ensuring that both foreign workers and their sponsors stick to their employment intentions once they have entered Australia.

Our universities and other places of further education are also chasing the Asian student dollar, because these institutions are no longer sustainable on the basis of government funding and HECS payments.

The types of employment for which we lack sufficient skills, as listed in the schedules on the Department of Immigration's website, is disturbing. Many are basic occupations—an inconvenient fact that has a flow-on effect of leading to regional difficulties in the obtaining of sufficient workers. And yet importing foreign workers in circumstances where rural youth unemployment may be as high as 20 per cent is a bandaid solution.

As a regulatory measure, a number of regional bodies have been established to certify that there are insufficient workers available to meet the market's requirements in particular occupations. It would be an interesting exercise for the federal auditor-general to audit the certification-justification process and the notification rates of workers who leave their sponsored work without first notifying Immigration. The sponsoring employer doesn't seem to have this obligation.

The problem of foreign workers is a global concern. If they displace local workers at lower cost, and also create an additional burden on our social-service facilities, they are not part of our migration solution. Our social services are much kinder and more permanent than those operating in most countries.

We must have migrants. It is good for us and good for them if they become Australians who retain and acquire the best practices of both their old society and ours. Virtually all of us are the children of people who migrated to Australia in the twentieth century.

I think that foreign workers are, at best, a temporary policy-solution. They are also a distraction from the main task of encouraging migration.

My fear is that this temporary solution may lead to the creation of an underclass of the kind obvious in other countries. Australian egalitarianism is not something we should lightly surrender.

Guest workers are often in the news because they have been exploited by their employers. In the absence of any other demonstrable motivation, the only reason for us bringing in guest workers is to pay them less and give them poorer working conditions than locals are entitled to. This is happening in an environment where our employment model is under severe stress and it is likely that some people will have to work longer than they had planned or expected.

Offshoring is another 'solution' that has crept up on our society. The concept of overseas call centres is relatively new. Originally heralded as a great solution to the problem of unemployment in rural and outer-suburban areas, call centres seem to have been moved offshore in recent times to reduce labour costs and overheads. The result has usually been a decline in customer service, or the sort of sales harassment that led to the Do Not Call legislation being passed by the federal government.

Innovation

Innovation is the government's panacea for growing the Australian economy, but it won't fix up our economy by itself.

Innovation is one of those words that can mean different things, or even nothing at all, to the individual listener. Literally meaning 'to make new', it's generally used to refer to ways of performing a business process better, creating a new, more efficient, or attractive product, or simply making an existing product more useful or attractive to the consumer.

But there has to be a more sophisticated and pervasive long-term approach to the global financial disaster than simply saying that we have to do better.

China didn't come to dominate the world market for consumer goods by innovating. Not to put too fine a point on it, all of its manufacturing processes and product development were stolen, copied, or imported. It gave multinational companies favourable taxation and other concessions — with the Chinese labour-cost a huge attraction — until it could appropriate or transfer the technology and know-how. Very few successful Western companies in China will stay successful or Western.

It starts to get difficult when a small country like Australia is told constantly that it must innovate. We don't know how — and for good reason. The low-hanging fruit of innovation was picked off long ago by companies desperate to remain in business. Others that are protected by non-tariff barriers have remained committed to their tried-and-true approach to the delivery of products and services.

How can the miners innovate? Of course, they could try going down the track of adding value to their exports of ores and primary shapes — but the government has never encouraged this sort of innovation because it involves risk.

How will our agriculture sector innovate? It faces the same dilemma as the miners. Further processing agricultural produce involves the taking-on of risk and a need for extra capital. There is plenty of the former and not much of the latter around today.

How will the public servants (which includes the teachers, the road and rail employees, the police, the health workers, those in councils, and the carers at home or in private hospitals) innovate? Will our society accept innovations that reduce the fundamental cost-structures of these industries and their employment levels?

If we are prepared to accept the consequences of this type of innovation, it can be achieved. The banks and Telstra have been innovating by reducing or offshoring their workforce for some time.

Manufacturing has traditionally been the heartland of innovation. The difficulty is that the leaders and innovators in the sector have not been encouraged to think that there is any future for manufacturing in Australia. Government procurement policy has generally moved past the so-called level playing field.

This is changing under the Rudd government. The Minister for Innovation, Industry, Science and Research, Senator Kim Carr, has been a staunch advocate for manufacturing, but has come under heavy fire in cabinet for what are regarded as protectionist views. The prime minister acknowledged in parliament on 13 March 2008 that the current-account deficit was one of the five great problems in the Australian economy.

Why would an innovative manufacturer in Australia not sell their new product to a global marketer, and take the money and run? The chances are that he or she will never get the money necessary within Australia to develop a global market, and that their development will be pirated in five minutes flat. Global companies have the financial and political resources to avoid such a fate.

The Sarich engine is a prime example. The Perth inventor Ralph Sarich invented a passenger car engine that was a massive advance on the technology of 35 years ago, which led to a number of engine and ancillary-equipment revisions that were very successful. The inventor made a lot of money by selling his intellectual property to multinational manufacturers.

It is not sufficient to invent a better mousetrap. The government has to support marketing in both Australia and overseas. It needs to rethink its approach to procurement. Otherwise it is almost impossible for Australian companies to move from invention to dissemination, and then to maturity in the market place. They simply can't raise the capital, and are seduced by a big payday for their developments.

The implantable Cochlear ear may be an exception that proves the rule. Usually, Australia has been unable to commercialise such high-technology inventions. And now, in our current economic climate, floating a public company to develop such a product — the demand for which is unknowable initially — is not a likely road to success.

Only one sector of our economy has been truly innovative: retail, which employs over one million people. Its willingness to accept imports and to focus on part-time employment has been a major innovation that has reduced costs and increased profits. Its practices have delivered such a level of employment flexibility that retailers are able to tailor their workforces to meet the cloth of consumer demand.

I suppose the big question is, how do we foster innovation across the Australian economy and the national workforce? How do we make the doctors and lawyers and the services sector more innovative and productive? The finance sector has certainly been innovative, but it hasn't been productive.

Innovation that reduces employment in the services sector, which we are told constitutes more than 80 per cent of the Australian workforce, will not generate efficiencies that expand the economy.

The theoretical argument is that innovation reduces prices, increases consumer demand, and creates a requirement for more employment. In practice, this isn't what happens all or even most of the time. Industry has a habit of appropriating cost-reductions as additional profit.

There is a huge difference between great theories and their practical application. Dissemination — whether in the spread of newly invented products and services, or simply in the sprucing up of old products and services — has always been harder and more costly to achieve than invention.

A lot of people have jumped on the innovation bandwagon. They have had the usual Eureka moment and are committed to change. I would love to believe that innovation is the path out of our present crisis, but the reality is that most people are wary of change. It's not sufficient to say that they shouldn't be. We always want to think that change is achievable and fast, but life is not that simple.

We are still feeling the impact of free-market theory on our global economy. The free-market economists have had their day, and the next horde of management consultants, researchers, and academic innovators is about to descend on us. It would be good to take a collective breath, and try to understand the consequences of yet another one-shot solution to our woes. Our economic problems are more complex and pragmatic than that.

Innovation is good, but it always creates social and economic costs—and it takes time to implement. Our really big problem is, how do we employ all of those part-time employees or new service-sector employees who will be out of work shortly? Innovation won't save them.

We need to help people understand what innovation can do for families and for the Australian economy. Until now, it has been a nebulous buzzword that doesn't mean anything in particular to most people. Repeating a word over and over doesn't make it meaningful. Nor does it make it true.

Food or finance for Asia

The Productivity Commission devoted one of its annual reports to the notion that Australia should become the food basket of Asia. This was a nice idea, but we have already had trouble selling rice and beef to the Japanese, and beef to the Koreans. The USAFTA was supposed to be a major winner for the beef industry. (As we have seen, sugar was excluded from the start—funny about that.)

There have been various state government initiatives designed to turn us into a financial centre for Asia. The Chinese, the Japanese, and the rest of Asia probably thought that was a great joke.

Invest Australia: attracting vulture capital and assisting elite workers

One of the great scourges of the modern day is the availability of footloose capital, whose owners have no commitment to anything other than short-run profit maximisation. They arrive like a locust plague and depart overnight, leaving nothing of long-run benefit to the economy.

During the era of the Howard government, there was an industry-policy coup that most of us didn't even know about, when an entity known as Invest Australia was born in 1997. Between July 2002 and March 2007, it was responsible for 357 projects, generating $55 billion and 27,000 jobs. The government assistance given to foreign companies recommended by Invest Australia was specifically directed to firms that wouldn't invest in Australia unless they were given government funds, and that would leave as soon as the flow of government funds stopped. These weren't just any jobs. Invest Australia said that investment in Australia is 'most of all a decision to access our most valuable asset—Australia's elite pool of highly educated, skilled and multilingual people'.

Who decided that multilingual, double-degree, or higher-degree graduate workers were our most valuable asset? This was academic elitism gone mad. What proportion of the population did they represent? Why are a couple of degrees or a higher degree a demonstration of the value of a worker? This really did ignore the reality of the market place and the enormous range of qualities and experiences that create a workforce asset.

For a start, most of the people with two or more degrees are usually accountants, lawyers, consultants, or researchers. They don't create businesses, and their CVs are certainly not the most common qualifications of CEOs in big or medium-sized businesses. This type of nonsense was part of Australia's problem, not the solution.

This policy involved the blunt reversal of 30 years of neutral resource-allocation policy in government. Invest Australia was about picking winners in a secret process, and giving them public money as an incentive to come to Australia. This was supposedly anathema to the neo–liberals — unless, that is, they were the ones selecting the winners.

Invest Australia's major publication (with a foreword by prime minister Howard and the then-minister for industry, resources and commerce) declared:

> The Australian Government is not disposed towards providing across the board incentives. The government does, however, acknowledge that in some circumstances there may be a need for specific incentives to be provided to secure strategic investments for Australia.

Invest Australia declared:

> Australia protects its investors. The country is ranked third in the world and first in the Asia Pacific region for significantly protecting shareholders rights. In terms of intellectual property, the patent and copyright enforcement regime is ranked second in the region.

It seems that we had a new protectionism, out of sight of the rest of us. It was designed to protect our most valuable asset, the 'elite' workers in the services sector.

Assistance requests were sent to Invest Australia and had to meet their internally generated criteria. The first criterion was that the project would not come to Australia unless it were to receive government assistance. How footloose is this?

The decision process was secret. A person called the Strategic Investment Co-ordinator advised the Department of Prime Minister and Cabinet, and he or she decided whether or not to provide incentives for a project. This was obviously not subject to public scrutiny and debate, which was the very reason that the Tariff Board was created in 1921. The Labor government duly transferred Invest Australia from Kim Carr's Department of Innovation to Austrade. Since then, it has effectively been disbanded.

Whether they like it or not, governments are populist. They represent the people. They ought not to be focused on the elite, which is able to look after itself.

The real issue is whether or not Invest Australia is alive and well under the Rudd government, or whether it has been consigned to the scrap heap of losers picked by the neo-liberals.

Compulsory superannuation

In Australia, we have allowed thousands of industry, professional, and private superannuation funds to pop up in what has to be the most inefficient manner possible. A full-scale inquiry into the superannuation industry, headed by Jeremy Co-oper, was initiated by the government in late 2009, with a completion date of mid-2010. As the deputy chairman of ASIC, Co-oper had helped that body change from a toothless tiger to an efficient regulatory power after the $5 billion HIH Insurance liquidation.

The global financial disaster has delivered a tremendous blow to the superannuation funds, which have lost over a hundred billion dollars. Their losses are likely to be in the order of between 20 and 30 per cent of their total fund holdings. They expect to make money in the future, but I don't understand how this can make up for the money they have lost. Even if the Australian stock market does climb back, that won't recover past losses. And how do we know whether or not they were visited by Merrill Lynch or Lehman Brothers, flogging CDOs to them?

The Future Fund

This is a very dangerous piece of government intervention. Sixty billion dollars of our money was handed by the Howard government to a top-heavy group of 30 people to play with. Headed by David Murray, retired CEO of the Commonwealth Bank, it was supposed to invest the money to create sufficient returns to cover the deficiency in Commonwealth superannuation that was created in the late 1990s.

The fund states on its website: 'Legislation stipulates that money cannot be drawn from the Future Fund until 2020 except for the purposes of meeting operating costs or unless the Future Fund's balance exceeds the target asset level as defined by the Future Fund Act.'

In 2007–08, the fund achieved earnings of 1.54 per cent, against its target return of 9.0–10.0 per cent. (Its target is CPI plus 4.5 per cent to 5.5 per cent, and the CPI in that year was

4.5 per cent.) It has lost money since its inception.

In October 2008, the Future Fund disclosed that it had lent money to Westpac, the National Australia Bank, and the ANZ Bank, but only the amount lent to ANZ was disclosed—$500 million. The fund had $34 billion in cash lodged with the Australian banks, so it couldn't have been making much money on those assets. The question is, how much has it lost in the global financial disaster, and how much has it lost by supporting Australian banks with such substantial cash deposits? This is a time when it should have been making money in the global financial market place, because cash was at an absolute premium. The Future Fund had lots of cash, but lent much of it to the banks to support them during the freeze on loan funds.

Blah, blah, blah: the New Economy, the Services Economy, the Global Economy, the Free-Market Economy, and the Information Economy

There is no doubt that we have massively expanded services and the information sector in the past 30 years. But you can't eat or wear services and information. The information-technology revolution owes nothing to free-market economics.

The services sector was bloated by the introduction of compulsory superannuation and the great bull market of 1998 to 2008, which introduced a lot of non-punters to the joys of share trading. The banking system grew enormously as a consequence of the trade in derivatives, especially for foreign currencies.

A lot of the services-sector growth claimed was also the result of statistical misrepresentation. As manufacturers and major import/export businesses grew, they decided that their core activities should not include moving, storing, packing, and unpacking the articles that they produced or imported. Coles and Woolworths and other major companies ran fleets of delivery vehicles and warehouses, and employed an army of Customs brokers and logistics managers; over time, these functions were outsourced.

THE PRODUCTIVITY COMMISSION LIBRARY

Finally, since 1996, the greatest area of growth in employment and national income has been in the retail, health-care and social assistance, and hospitality and entertainment industries. And yet, it could be argued that this growth has hindered Australia's economic development and prosperity. It is concealing the true character of the occupations and remuneration of much of our workforce. It is making a mockery of the concept of continuous training and innovation.

In the health-care and social-welfare sector, we have created poor houses for the old who don't own a home to live in. These properties give employment to the poor and to recent migrants.

In February 2009, the retail sector employed nearly 1.2 million people, and health care and social assistance employed a further 1.15 million people. The services sector contributed 65 per cent of Australian GDP in 2007–08.

The major problems I have with this sector of the economy is the falsity of its employment numbers, and the puff given to what is, in reality, often discretionary or even wasteful expenditure by consumers. For example, gambling, pubs, and clubs are a substantial contributor to the service sector's employment and revenue aggregates. The sector tends to employ the poor; older women rejoining the workforce; and unskilled workers, students, and recent migrants.

Probably more than 70 per cent of the employment recorded in these industries is for fewer hours than the workers wish to work. The hours are often discretionary — and it is the employer who exercises the discretion.

An employer can tell bar staff to go home after two hours, or not to bother coming in at all on a slow, wet week; in retail outlets, the packers and the checkout people often work in four-hour shifts. And part-time employees are the first people to be retrenched. The reason is obvious: the employer owes them nothing.

Part-time workers receive an amount per hour that theoretically includes an allowance for sick leave, and holiday and other entitlements. Those amounts are generally less than $20 an hour. According to the Australian Bureau of Statistics, we have three million part-time employees, and half of them would like to work more hours. It should be noted that part-time workers who work more than an hour a week are regarded by the government statistician as being employed. This sleight-of-hand enabled the Howard government to make the fundamental but false claim that we had full employment in Australia.

In December 2009, our unemployment rate was 5.5 per cent, but there were over 7.5 per cent of part-time employees in our 12 million-strong labour market who wanted to work more hours.

Last and least: tariff reductions

Amazingly, there are still some calls being made for further tariff reductions—against a background of the average tariff rate in Australia now being 3 per cent, and over 75 per cent of goods being free of duty, either at their substantive rate or through the by-law system. The only items with 10 per cent rates are textiles, footwear, and clothing, while motor vehicles and components are now dutiable at 5 per cent.

For the first ten years after I left the Industries Assistance Commission, I worked as a tariff consultant representing major importers and their associations. We also made a lot of money preparing tariff-concession applications and undertaking tariff audits for very large companies. These included Woolworths and Coles, who are probably the country's largest importers. I still remember the methodology and the detail of the application of Australia's tariff regime over the past 30 years.

This point underpins the critical comments that follow. The Productivity Commission and its antecedents, the consultants employed by the Department of Foreign Affairs and Trade and, in May 2009, the Centre for International Economics (which measured the benefits of trade liberalisation) do not know what they are talking about when they purport to measure the benefit to the consumer of the tariff-reductions that have occurred over the past 30 years.

This calculation was a constant piece of misinformation published by the commission in its passenger motor-vehicle industry reports. It was used deliberately to convince government that the benefit that would be provided to consumers from tariff reductions could be reduced to a dollar amount per vehicle.

Economists have continued the practice by accepting (along with their assumptions) the various input-output models churned out by economists, who have made tens of millions of dollars (basically paid by government) by selling the resulting information to the Department of Foreign Affairs and Trade and their free-market consultants.

The models began with ORANI. Other models quoted by the Centre for International Economics and used in their simulations include the CIEG-Cubed, the GTAP, and the AUS-M models.

These meaningless collections of letters are a classic example of how to obfuscate and to deceive the public by reference to a supposed authority (in this case, various econometric models) that cannot be understood by most people and which leave out fundamental variables. The unknown, unmeasured, and excluded variables include such essential facts as the following:

- Tariff reductions do not have to be passed on, and they generally aren't. As we have seen, the major concern of the importers group of the Federal Chamber of Automotive Industries was that the government — after the tariff reductions that were imposed following the 1991 Industry Commission Inquiry into motor vehicles — would force importers and retailers to pass on the cost benefit arising from the duty reduction. They didn't do so, and the cost benefit was not passed on.

- All tariffs are calculated on Customs values for duty, which follow precisely the valuation legislation contained in the Customs Act 1901, and illuminated since then by a number of cases in the Administrative Appeals Tribunal, the Federal Court, the full bench of the Federal Court and, occasionally, the High Court. The Customs value (which roughly approximates to the selling price from the exporter to the importer, excluding ocean and air freight and insurance) is rarely more than half the retail price — and some retailers (for example, cosmetics retailers) mark up their retail sales price by 700 per cent.

In this context, it is especially ludicrous to think — as the Productivity Commission and most commentators in the media do — that eliminating a duty of 5 or 10 per cent will have any impact whatsoever in the market place. All that this tokenism achieves is to slightly reduce government revenue collections and enrich exporters and/or the supply chain by the same amount.

- Retail prices of imports are not established on the basis of landed, duty-paid costs, into-store costs plus administrative and selling expenses, plus a gross margin. They are based on what the market will bear.
- The tariff-rate research methodology of the models is focused on tariffs. It does not include any analysis of tariff concessions (which reduce the duty rate to zero), which have operated since 1983, replacing a by-law system that had been in operation since 1927. It does not include specific concessions such as policy by-laws, which have also featured in the tariff system since the early 1970s.

The Centre for International Economics states that 'the causes of the Global Financial Crisis are complex'. The calculation of a household dollar-benefit of $3900 from tariff reductions in the past 20 years is more than complex. It is inaccurate and, in fact, impossible to calculate or investigate unless you are privy to Customs values and corresponding retail prices. The problems of empirical calculation have never been intelligently or empirically addressed by the economic consultancy think-tanks or the modellers. They just keep dishing up what their free-trade audience wants to hear.

The tariff debate is well and truly dead, and yet the high-tariffs corpse keeps being dug up and paraded for various political purposes. There has been value in reducing tariffs. But we have been naive not to introduce non-tariff barriers.

Measuring the Extent of the Damage

The Rudd government has spent a lot of money on stimulus measures, but it has been less profligate than countries such as the US and Britain. Most of the quantum of our major budget-deficit projections and debt for the next five years is a consequence of expected reductions in taxation collections and the commitment to previously announced major infrastructure expenditures.

The media and our commentators have concentrated heavily on Australia's good fortune to date. Confidence is a natural and powerful stimulant, and we generally dislike prophets of doom. Politicians and the media tend to dismiss negative comments about the future.

The global financial disaster is likely to be the biggest setback to our standard of living, our employment prospects, and our savings that we have experienced in our lifetimes. It is reckless to diminish its potential and to treat with indifference that which is gradually unfolding in the world economy. It is an event so important to Australia that we must take action to try to eliminate or at least minimise its consequences. We cannot afford to do nothing.

One of Australia's greatest perils has been the refusal of government and industry watchdogs—such as the Australian Prudential Regulation Authority and the Australian Securities and Investments Commission—to force individual companies and associations, and clubs and councils, to disclose the extent of their losses. We are currently in a lull not unlike the Phoney War in the months before World War II started in earnest. For example, the banks have used government guarantees to raise $100 billion. Why are they raising so much money if, as they have stated, their losses have been modest?

We have been damaged in a number of very specific, but often hidden, ways. This appendix provides a brief year-to-year comparison of the performances of what are often cited as the major indicators of the state of the Australian economy: employment; share-value capitalisation; major consumer durables; income; government expenditure; superannuation and pensions; education; social security, services, and charities; and research and development.

Employment

Our unemployment level has increased from 4 per cent to 5.5 per cent as at December 2009, and was projected to reach 6 per cent in 2009–10. This may not happen, but it is more about the Bureau of Statistics' methodology than the reality. The unemployment percentage would be much higher if people wishing to work more hours were included in the calculation. They have been counted as employed full time since the early days of the coalition government.

A WEALTHY ECONOMIST TOASTS HIS RETIREMENT AFTER A LIFE DEVOTED TO A FAILED AND RUINOUS THEORY

A MODESTLY PAID FACTORY WORKER IS SACKED AFTER A LIFE DEVOTED TO ACTUALLY MAKING SOMETHING

FREE TRADE

The Australian Bureau of Statistics calculated that the level of under-utilised labour hours was sitting at 13.4 per cent of standard working hours for the present labour force. This is a new measure, and it had risen by more than 3 per cent in the previous year.

The ABS surveys are based on a sampling of less than 2 per cent of the workforce. I wonder how well the new measurement sample picks up the major part-time job losses that have occurred in the gaming, hotel, and hospitality industries, or the changes that have taken place in retail part-time employment. The government's cash splash (as the opposition called it) may have delayed part-time job losses in significant part-time employment sectors such as retailing and entertainment.

Accepting part-time employment and having two or three incomes per household have become part of our strategy to maintain our standard of living. There is no doubt that many Australian families will have lower incomes in the short term, at least. It is very likely that they will rely on their access to savings and credit cards to maintain their standard of living when their combined income has been reduced. The slump in consumer spending will occur when their reserves are seriously depleted.

Shares

The total share-value loss in Australia is relatively easy to calculate, but is generally shown as a number that has no meaning. The Australian Stock Exchange provides a figure called the All Ordinaries (All Ords) Price Index, which is what the media use for their daily reports on whether the market is up or down. Data is also available from the exchange detailing the total market capitalisation of listed companies.

In October 2007, the market peaked at an All Ords index level of 6779. At the time, the market capitalisation of listed companies totalled $1,643 billion.

In February 2009, the market bottomed at 3296, or less than half of the index's peak. The listed-company market capitalisation was then $888 billion, or 54 per cent of its peak value. This meant that as much as $750 billion had been wiped off the portfolio values of Australians owning shares directly or through their superannuation funds.

At the time of writing, in late January 2010, the index was around 4700, and the market capitalisation of listed companies was back over $1 billion. This is still around $600 billion down on its peak—over 40 per cent of Australia's national income.

The major strategy employed by many substantial listed companies that have been savagely wounded but not completely destroyed by the global financial disaster has been to issue shares at a substantial discount to the prices paid by existing shareholders. They always nominate the value—they certainly don't let the market decide the price of their capital raising—and used this technique to issue a record $90 billion worth of such shares in the 2008–09 financial year.

This money has captured much of the pool of investment funds available for the stock market, and has caused a major dilution of the value of shares (which had already been hit hard by the stock-market fall), as well as an expansion of the total number of a company's shares (which is the divisor for dividends). In taking such action, the companies have been selling the concept that they are 'repairing' their balance sheets. But very little explanation is provided regarding the reasons for the repair having been needed in the first place. In fact, the 'repairs' are often a consequence of overseas borrowings or company takeovers that were indulged in at the wrong price before the global crisis started.

The simple reality attending the plethora of share issues is that existing shareholders are watching the price of their shares fall to match the bargain-basement prices offered to fill the new share issues. Shareholders are losing a large slice of their capital value immediately, and can look forward to the prospect of the relevant company earnings being spread over a much larger share base. This will obviously reduce earnings—and dividends—per share.

Major market indicators

All of the following statistics have been taken from the Reserve Bank of Australia's statistical appendices, which generally begin in 1959. This is a straightforward but enormously comprehensive database for a wide range of indicators and measures of movements in major financial markets and in the Australian economy in general.

Car sales

From April 2007 to March 2008, motor vehicle sales were 1,063,400. In the corresponding period for 2008–2009, sales were 957,800—a reduction of more than 100,000 vehicle sales. The new-car and after-sales market is worth $30 billion, so a 10 per cent reduction would have cost the industry $3 billion.

Car sales in December 2009 boomed as advantage was taken of the government's very generous stimulus measure of a 50 per cent tax deduction of the cost of buying a vehicle for business purposes—even including passenger vehicles. Nevertheless, the industry has forecast that the level of vehicle production in Australia in 2010 will be the lowest total since 1957. Ford Australia is likely to stop manufacturing the Ford Falcon, as the company has decided to produce a global car.

Housing approvals

For the same 2007–08 period, housing approvals were 157,200. In 2008–09, the total number approved was 134,000. The reduction of 23,200 housing approvals meant a reduction in revenue for the building industry of the order of $4.5 billion.

According to preliminary figure supplied by the Housing Industry Association, housing approvals in 2009 fell by 14 per cent compared to 2008.

Retail sales

Retail sales held up from 2007–08 to 2008–09; in fact, they increased by 3 per cent at current prices. This may simply reflect price increases and the impact of the Rudd government's cash injection on sales in December and January, which were noticeably up. However, by the July–December half of 2009, the absence of fresh government-stimulus money and the imposition of interest-rate increases started to weaken retail sales; in fact, seasonally adjusted sales fell by 0.7 per cent in December, and rose by only 0.4 per cent for the whole December half. The retail market earned revenues of $237 billion in 2009.

Government expenditure

The government forecast that it would receive $30 billion less in revenue over the three financial years beginning in 2008–09 compared with the benchmark year of 2007–08. This suggests that Australia's national income will contract by about $150 billion over those three years from the level that was expected to have been achieved had the global disaster not happened. The extraordinary stimulus expenditure in the 2008–09 year, and commitments already made for the future, have already generated a public debt of $200 billion. This number is expected to rise to over $300 billion as the government continues to spend to fulfil its commitments for both infrastructure development and climate-change legislation.

That doesn't leave much for any future increases in government expenditure to stimulate the economy if it turns out that we are in a double-dip global recession.

Superannuation and pensions

Finding out the truth about our superannuation losses is not an easy matter. The Australian Prudential Regulation Authority is the industry's regulatory authority, and it is the subject of a major government inquiry. APRA's most recent report was released in December 2009, and covered the period from September 2008 to September 2009. An earlier report for the year ended June 2007 was revised in June 2009.

APRA oversees about 75 per cent of the nation's superannuation funds. Here are some highlights from APRA's most recent report:

- Contributions to all funds totalled $167 billion in 2006–07 and $119 billion in 2007–08.
- Total assets decreased in value by 2.1 per cent in the year ended 2007–08 (or about $20 billion).
- This also means that total contributions for the year lost value. This brought the total loss for the year to about $140 billion.
- There were 694,000 resignations from APRA

funds, but 559,000 of these people reinvested in other eligible rollover funds (most of which would have been APRA-supervised funds.)

- The biggest losers were super funds.
- From September 2008 to September 2009, losses were continuing. Actual assets increased in value from $749 billion to $769 billion (but there would have been after at least $80 billion worth of contributions in that period).
- The Howard government's 'Better Super Funds' taxation concession initiative, which allowed voluntary contributions of a million dollars per person in the first half of 2007, caused a spike in the contribution amount to $64 billion for that quarter, or twice the usual quarterly level.

Super funds would undoubtedly have benefited to some extent from preferred access at discounted prices to capital raisings and from buying shares at the bottom of the market. But I wouldn't hold out much hope for the sixty-something baby boomers whose super assets have fallen by more than one-third in value, unless they are planning to work until they are seventy-five.

Long-run costs

We will be paying for the global disaster for a long time to come. There are decisions being made now by families about whether to buy a house or have another child. For those who are newly unemployed or are working fewer hours, or who will shortly become unemployed, the likely response will be to delay decisions that create significant financial obligations. Increases in unemployment levels for both full-time and part-time workers will have a multiplier effect for consumer purchases as the reduced spending of the unemployed and underemployed impacts upon the market for goods and services. Those who are working are already saving more than they have in the past ten years.

These personal decisions and attitudes must have a profound effect upon the government's central goals of increasing productivity through innovation, and creating a mobile, constantly self-educating workforce. Small businesses will not have the money to invest in research and development.

Education in Australia has become a very expensive process, and the burden of the cost has shifted fundamentally onto the education consumers — the students. We are dumbing down Australian education, especially at international colleges for international students. The problem is insinuating itself into our major universities. The result is that we are reducing the value of our quality education brand name to obtain export income in the short term.

For the first time ever, an economic global event has penetrated the minds of the population in general. The Depression of the 1930s may have been more severe in its financial impact, but most people didn't have the education or the exposure to media to know and understand its global extent. This time, the subject is in the media every day.

The additional government burden in the long run will be in social security, education, and aged care. We are already developing a HECS-funding overhang of billions of dollars that will never be paid by students who drop out or leave the country. This will be revealed as another unfunded liability for the states and the nation when the accountants eventually get around to bringing the loss onto the balance sheets of government.

At present we still have savings, and we are only just beginning to experience the feeling of not being free to buy anything that appeals to us. We can see the bottom of the money bin.

As people spend their savings and lose their jobs, they will increasingly rely on social security. The size of the decline in superannuation funds and share-market losses means that most of us will work longer — or, if we can't, we will rely more on the federal government.

Charities and other philanthropic organisations, which bear a large part of the social-welfare cost in Australia, simply won't receive the level of donations that they need to achieve their admirable goals.

The Rudd government is thinking about the long term, but it still needs to win elections in the short term. This explains why the economic forecasts in the 2009–10 budget were very pessimistic for the following three financial years, but then morphed into highly optimistic future increases in the gross domestic product. This was a well-tested tactic of never over-promising in forecasts that relate to near-term periods. Any over-achievement is then regarded as wonderful news.

The growth predictions for 2012–13 onwards will also be likely to coincide with another federal election, which the Rudd government may not be a certainty to win, given the gloomy outlook for the next few years.

If all the financial losses from all the losers we have relied on are added together, the total impact of the global financial disaster upon our lives becomes a lot clearer. We have to deal with diminished superannuation benefits, company asset-values and dividends, jobs, future government expenditures, housing values, educational opportunities … the list goes on. We will not be saved by a minerals boom, a services-sector revolution, or a leap forward in technology.

We need to rethink the approach to our economy. Free-market economics has to be discarded. We simply can't afford to keep facilitating rogue developments in the dark that destroy our economic stability when they are finally exposed to the light. In the past 30 years, we have changed from a country that makes the majority of things we need, to a country that imports the majority of things we use.

The fundamental questions facing our society are how we change and when. We should not cling to the past.

A Plain-English Glossary of Relevant Terms and Names

The Australian Prudential Regulation Authority (APRA)
The government body responsible for regulating, supervising, and monitoring banks, insurance companies, and superannuation funds.

Australian Customs Service
The government body responsible for all imports and exports, cross-border control, and border protection.

Australian Bureau of Statistics
Collects all statistics relevant to the Australian economy and for Australia in general.

***Ad valorem* rates**
Duty rates expressed as percentages and calculated on Customs value of imported goods.

Australian Taxation Office
Collects all personal taxes, company taxes, GST, and other taxes.

Balance of payments
The aggregate of all payments for transactions between residents of Australia and residents of the rest of the world, including payments for transactions in goods and services, and income paid and received.

Balance of trade
The aggregate of all payments for transactions between residents of Australia and the rest of the world for goods and services.

Bretton Woods Agreement
An agreement between the US, Britain, and Russia in 1947 to establish a system of global monetary management and exchange-rate stability. A number of international reforms, including Customs global systems, came from Bretton Woods.

Bilateral Trade agreements
Agreements between two countries providing specific trade-barrier concessions.

Blast furnaces
Furnaces that use coal to melt iron ore and various chemicals at temperatures up to 1200 centigrade iron to make iron and steel blooms, billets, and slabs.

Billions and trillions
A billion is a thousand million. A trillion is a million million. The ratio is the same as one day to three years to three thousand years.

Centre for International Economics

Economic consultancy used by Australian government for USAFTA and tariff-reduction studies.

Current-account deficit

An account is published monthly by the ABS aggregating all purchases and sales of goods and services occurring between residents of Australia and residents of the rest of the world. To that account is added payments and receipts for intellectual property, intangibles, and other assets of monetary value. The account may be in surplus or deficit. Australia's current account has been in deficit for the past 23 years. The total of those deficits is the foreign debt.

Collateralised Debt Obligations (CDOs)

A bundle of assets (such as mortgages and asset-backed loans) that carry different levels of cost, risks, and returns. When either interest or principal payments are made, they are made from the highest category (called a tranche) where there is less risk of default.

Container storage yards

Used to store empty containers prior to their return overseas.

Customs brokerage

Globally, all imports and exports are controlled by national Customs authorities. Their processes for duty calculation, valuation, and classification are based on a complex process derived from the Bretton Woods Agreement. Most importers and exporters use service providers to manage the interface with Customs.

Comptometers
Calculation machines that were the precursor to electronic calculators.

Customs bond stores
Secure premises under Customs control for the storage of goods that have not been duty paid.

Customs duties
Percentage-based (*ad valorem*) or specific (dollar amount per quantity) calculations, or combinations of both, used as the basis of Customs duty collection.

Double-tax treaties
Treaties between Australia and about 150 countries detailing taxation rates for withholding taxes on services, interest, and intellectual-property income transferred between countries.

Department of Foreign Affairs and Trade
Represents Australia internationally to deliver government policy and national interest goals in security, foreign and trade policy. Provides consular and passport services.

Department of Prime Minister and Cabinet
Policy advisers to the prime minister and cabinet on all domestic and international issues. Co-ordinates advice from other departments when the issues overarch a number of portfolios.

Dumping duties
A global protective measure designed to offset sales of goods internationally at prices lower than those in the supplier's home market.

Equilibrating tariffs

Until 1970, tariffs were usually imposed that equalled the difference between local industry prices and the landed price of imported goods.

Economic rationalism

Tariff or other border-protection mechanisms established on the basis of reasoned analysis and factual data rather than on the basis of self-interest, emotion, or ignorance of the basic policy purpose of assisting Australian value-added processes.

Econometric models

Inclusion of a number of variables in a formula that are governed by assumptions that are relevant for the purposes of the model. The variables' values are then changed to assess or support either predictive or policy outcomes.

Free-trade agreements

Bilateral agreements between countries that reduce tariffs and other protective mechanisms for some products.

Free-market economics

The theory that government should not intervene in markets unless there is demonstrable market failure.

Future Fund

A fund established in 2006 with part of budget surpluses to strengthen the financial position of the Australian government and enable it to meet unfunded Commonwealth superannuation liabilities in future years.

Gross domestic product (GDP)
The aggregate market price of all final goods and services made in Australia in a year.

Gross national product (GNP)
The market price of all final goods and services made in Australia and in overseas countries by Australian entities or individuals in a year.

Industries Assistance Commission
The name of the Productivity Commission in the 1970s and part of the 1980s.

Industries Commission
The name of the Productivity Commission in the late 1980s and early 1990s.

Institute of Public Affairs
A non-profit public policy think-tank supporting the free market of ideas, the free flow of capital, and limited and efficient government.

Low-doc mortgages
Loans made without any (or with very little) proof of income, assets, and debts or taxation returns. For businesses, annual financial statements are not required.

Merchandise trade
Imports and exports of physical goods and materials.

Multinationals, transnationals, global companies
Companies that trade across national borders. In most cases,

those companies establish market/distributor affiliates in overseas markets and only trade with them. They are called multinationals or transnationals.

Multilateral trade agreements
Trade agreements between a number of countries. The European Union operates under a multilateral trade agreement.

National income
The aggregation of payments to Australian residents for rents, salaries, and wages, interest, profit, acquisition of property or other assets, and for the acquisition of intangibles and intellectual property.

Non-tariff protection
Includes quotas, voluntary restraints, national product standards, packaging requirements.

ORANI model
An analytical framework and economy-wide database intended to answer questions regarding changes to other industries resulting from a change in the level of tariffs or other forms of assistance.

OECD
Organisation for Economic and Cultural Development. The international organisation which has established the transfer-pricing rules and methodologies that are used by all developed countries.

Productivity Commission
The successor commission to the Tariff Board and the Industries Commission.

Quarantine
Manages border control in respect of biological threats, animal and plant diseases, and human-health risks.

Quarantine place
Depots for inspecting, cleaning, or holding goods or containers for inspection to ensure that they do not breach quarantine regulations. A quarantine station may hold animals or people if their disease or infection is regarded as a risk.

Specific rates
A duty rate based on an amount per unit of measurement, such as $25 per litre of alcohol, or $2 per cubic metre of timber.

Tariff Board
The predecessor economic advisery body to the Productivity Commission. The board was established in 1921.

The Treasury
Advises government on monetary and fiscal policy, government spending and budget, tax, and retirement-income arrangements, financial systems, corporate practices, competitive impediments, consumer protection, and foreign investment.

Tops down or bottoms up
The alternatives of bringing tariffs down or up to create a benchmark for all tariff rates.

Transfer pricing
Cross-border prices for the transfer of goods and services, loans, and intellectual property between affiliates and affiliates and their parent company.

Transfer-pricing methodologies

OECD-agreed methods of calculating an arms' length price for transactions between affiliates.

Transfer-pricing documentation

Analysis of the functions, assets, and risks of a company trading with cross-border affiliates; supporting data for the choice of transfer-pricing methodology; and demonstration that the method has been applied by the company.

Tranches

Different categories of risk and value for securities bundled into collateralised debt obligations. The greater the risk and the higher the reward, the lower the tranche.

Unilateral trade liberalisation

The theory espoused by Alf Rattigan and Bill Carmichael (both chairmen of the Industries Assistance Commission) that Australia should not trade off tariff reductions, but reduce duty rates regardless of the actions of other countries.

World Trade Organisation

The global trade body that has more than 170 nation members. It pursues free trade in goods and services, but protects intellectual property. It is the international organisation responsible for dumping complaints.

Acknowledgements

I have spent my life writing long submissions and pieces of advice on industry policy and tax matters, and I have come from an environment where attractive assertions are almost the stock-in-trade of consultants. Writing a book, however, is an entirely different kettle of fish. Henry Rosenbloom, Scribe's publisher and my editor, has given me a new perspective of how to write, especially to do with the literary and factual precision that is necessary for a book. I thank him for providing me with a significant and valuable lesson in a field where I thought I knew what I was doing.

John Spooner has been my constant partner throughout fifteen years of articles, with cartoons that argued passionately against the free-market chorus in government and the media. His drawings often made the point more powerfully and lucidly than my words did. I thank him for his knowing commitment to an unpopular perspective, and for his friendship.

Any factual errors made or theoretical crimes committed in this book are, of course, my own fault.